NICHOLS ACADEMY:
THE SPRING ON THE HILL
1815~1931

Revised Edition

VOLUME I IN A BICENTENNIAL SERIES

JAMES L. CONRAD JR., PH.D.

PUBLISHED BY NICHOLS COLLEGE, 2008, 2014

PRINTED BY TIGER PRESS, EAST LONGMEADOW, MASSACHUSETTS

Published by Nichols College, 2008 [2014]
123 Center Road, Dudley, Massachusetts 01571

Printed in the United States of America
Book cover and design by Patricia Korch, Creative Director, Nichols College
Book interior production by Darcy Adshead, Adshead Graphics, Auburn, MA
Printed by Tiger Press, East Longmeadow, Massachusetts

ISBN 978-0-9815664-3-6

Cover: Nichols Academy Campus and Students (circa 1878).
Source: Untitled photograph. Courtesy Nichols College Archives.

TABLE OF CONTENTS

ILLUSTRATIONS

PREFACE TO THE REVISED EDITION

This edition contains material recently located in the Nichols College Archives. It has been added to Chapters 5 and 6. Chapter 5 was substantially changed and retitled "The Nature of Mr. Conant's Academy, 1874–1902," with new sections on "A New Purpose and Program" and "Life at the Academy in the 1880s." The title for Chapter 6 also has been changed somewhat while the chapter itself contains a new section titled "The Educational Efforts of the Academy and the Town." Added as well is a final section in Appendix C ("Nichols Academy Student Enrollment Numbers, 1819–1909") that was omitted in the first edition.

DEDICATION

This edition is dedicated to my wonderful wife, Bunny, who passed away
last summer. She was a longtime supporter of Nichols and a stalwart
of the Conrad family since she first worked at Nichols in 1950.

PREFACE

Educational history generally is seen as social and cultural history. In the case of Nichols Academy, it is local history as well. This book, *Nichols Academy: The Spring on the Hill, 1815–1931*, originally was written to be part of the bicentennial celebration of Nichols – Academy and College – in 2015. The special significance of the Academy's history, however, calls for separate and earlier publication. It was decided that this publication date should coincide with the celebration of Dudley's 275th Anniversary. The Academy's history also will be republished as part of the bicentennial history of Nichols that will cover the period from 1815 to 2015.

Beneath the Academy's history is the story of its archives that wandered from box to box and building to building until a proper, climate-controlled location was constructed in 2000. The boxes were opened and catalogued by Nichols Library Director Jim Douglas, and Acquisitions Librarian Evelyn Nieszczezewski. It then was possible to consider a formal history of Nichols.

The writing of Nichols Academy's history has received extensive help. It has been made possible by the commitment and generosity of Robert B. Kuppenheimer, Nichols College Class of 1969, and the support of the sixth president of Nichols College, Debra M. Townsley. Most helpful along the way have been Library Director, Jim Douglas, and a host of others at Nichols including Cynthia Brown, Diane Perry, Patricia Korch, Dorothy Millhofer, and Susan Veshi. This appreciation includes the contributions of members of the Nichols College History Project Committee who offered support and valuable insights. Others from the Dudley community who have assisted over time include Carol Ann Eaton, and Marion and Charles Moseley, true historians. My special thanks also go to Jack Larkin, President Townsley, Jim Douglas, Professor Daniel Ivascyn, Professor Thomas G. Smith, my longtime colleague at Nichols, and my wife, Bunny, who commented on draft versions. The remaining faults are mine alone.

INTRODUCTION

At the yearly graduation and reunion of Nichols Academy on June 17, 1886, the Reverend W. E. Knox of Webster, Massachusetts, remarked that booming manufacturing villages located in Webster and Dudley received their water power from "springs on the hills."[1] He favorably compared this power with the intellectual power he saw flowing from Nichols Academy, a hilltop "spring" situated on nearby Dudley Hill. Knox was touching on two vital ingredients of nineteenth century America's success: industrial growth and a supporting educational system. They formed a vital and natural partnership at a crucial point in time.

This is a history of a "spring" on a hill. Little has been written about the Dudley academy founded by Amasa Nichols in rural, south-central Massachusetts in 1815.[2] Nonetheless, its fascinating history forms the first era of an academic institution that ultimately touches three centuries on its way to two hundred years. This course reaches almost all levels and dimensions of the new nation's evolving educational experience. After closing its doors in 1909, the former academy campus was reorganized as a junior college in 1931 and then as a four-year college in 1958. In short, the history of Nichols Academy provides a well-grounded beginning for a unique and dynamic educational odyssey.

The term, "academy," probably had its origins around 375 B.C. in the meetings of Plato and his followers in an Athenian garden owned by Academus. With time, "academy" came to signify a group of scholars or professionals such as the American Academy of Arts and Sciences. Sometimes academies are associated with specific locations or unique purposes as in the case of America's military academies. Beginning in the mid-1700s, Americans frequently used this term to describe a school offering courses for students who had finished elementary school. Most academies offered what is now referred to as secondary education for students between the ages of twelve and twenty-two.

Academies became practical and important solutions for energetic and forward-looking Americans seeking additional education for their children during the first half of the nineteenth century and beyond.[3] Timothy Dwight, later president of then Yale College (1795–1817), observed that academies offered a dual curriculum serving both those destined for college and those who did not intend to go further.[4] This became an uniquely American approach to secondary education. In time, academies came to represent a specific era. By 1850, at least 1,007 out of more than 6,085 academies in the United States were located in New England.[5] Their numbers, however, started to decline when public high schools emerged just before the American Civil War. By the end of the nineteenth century, academy numbers had dwindled to the point where many in still young America believed these schools "had become a thing of the past."[6] Some academies had disappeared or were absorbed by public high school systems. Others continued as outstanding college preparatory schools. A few evolved into educational institutions beyond the secondary level; Nichols Academy in Dudley, Massachusetts, is included in this group.

Nichols Academy's long existence as a rural academy clearly qualifies it for special attention even though there are older institutions with significantly larger enrollments and greater endowments. Massachusetts schools such as Dummer Academy (now The Governor's Academy), Deerfield Academy, Groton (now Lawrence Academy), Milton Academy, and Phillips Academy in Andover are better known, but the experience of Nichols Academy founded in rural Dudley in 1815, was significantly different from other schools.[7] Nichols Academy was one of three former Massachusetts academies established before 1826 – Leicester in 1784, Bradford in 1803, and Nichols in 1815 – that later became colleges.[8]

One who spoke pridefully about the Nichols Academy experience was the Reverend Charles L. Goodell, D.D., a longtime Dudley Hill resident and a member of an illustrious Dudley family, many of whom attended the Academy just across the road from his home. Reverend Goodell, a nationally-known Methodist clergyman in the 1920s, eventually became president of the Nichols Academy Board of Trustees. His book, *Black Tavern Tales: Stories of Old New England*, reflects strong feelings for his old town and its academy. After fifty years of close association with Nichols Academy, he gracefully commented about its contributions:

> . . . the New England academy did more than any other agency, except the church, to develop the love for learning among the farmers and country folk. There was self-denial by father and mother, brother and sister to send at least one boy from the farm to college. . . . They climbed to the high places of opportunity and power through development which was possible to them by the training which the academy provided. It would be possible to name half a hundred men who had a college education because of the influence of Nichols Academy, which was situated in our little town.[9]

As Reverend Goodell saw it, the Academy was vital for the new society. Perhaps he was too laudatory, perhaps not. The accomplishments of academies during the first half of the nineteenth century became part of an unparalleled growth period in American society. To illustrate its contributions, one can point to its introduction and utilization of a diversified and evolving curriculum, the education of women as well as men, a respect for a humanist tradition, the training of common school teachers leading to overall improvement in the quality of local education, the strengthening of college preparation programs allowing the raising of college admission standards, and the introduction of scientific subjects in instructional areas.[10] The nineteenth century academy was the product of society's educational needs that had religious, economic and cultural origins. Nichols Academy continued to be an active and contributing educational institution until 1909 when increasing numbers of public high schools throughout Massachusetts, coupled with shifting local demographics, limited its enrollment and forced its closing.[11]

Historians have not ignored the place of academies in early American secondary education. Some picture the academy as part of a transitional era experienced as America moved toward modern democracy from colonial and imperial beginnings.[12] The academy is seen being replaced by the secular public high school as secondary education evolved toward the fulfillment of the American dream of equality and democracy in this linear view of American educational development.[13] Others place more emphasis on the relationship between the academy and the fundamentally rural environment in which it thrived. Many believe that the age of the academy ended with the arrival of the free public high school and the disappearance of a welcoming environment.[14]

But this view of the academy as a classic evolutionary stage in the history of American education is not shared by everyone. For instance, some have focused instead on a "persistence of educational attitudes and structures" long existing within the American system of education.[15] Such an approach sees American education acquiring its "fundamental characteristics" in the nineteenth century and believes there has been little change since.[16] A few others have provided necessary descriptive studies focusing on the operational features of old New England academies existing prior to 1826.[17]

Clearly the Dudley academy stands between the elitist Latin grammar school of colonial Massachusetts and the free public high school of the late nineteenth century. But it is more than that. Nichols Academy, as well as other similar academies, also must be understood as powerful transforming forces. Lives were changed because of academies. So too were their rural societies. There is a legacy here. Many young men and women in rural America received an education that placed them at the forefront of an increasingly dynamic and complex American society – and it took them away from the old hometown. Their leaving changed the nature of the rural world they left behind.

At the Academy, women had the opportunity to measure their intellectual abilities against men and develop new and specialized skills such as teaching that enabled them to take on new challenges, both inside and outside the rural village. Those who stayed at home did so with new opportunities to assist in community development with a better understanding of the processes that were at work beyond their towns. Colonial America had established tradition as a surefire guide for early rural inhabitants. A century later, academies such as Nichols offered education as a means of dealing with on-coming change – and then its students made significant contributions to its fabric.

Changes occurred in the operational course and institutional philosophy of Nichols Academy between 1815 and 1931, although the institution itself remained in the same location and worked with essentially the same age group. Its course and development provide the basis for the chapter structure that follows. The initial chapter describes the beginnings of the first academy under Amasa Nichols and the Universalists and explains the reasons why the Universalist academy did not continue beyond 1823. The second and third chapters focus on what is termed the "Old Academy" and provide substance for what can be called the "learning village." The fourth chapter cites new elements after 1865 that accelerated change in the Academy. This process included the activities of the state, the town, and of Hezekiah Conant, a former Academy student and Rhode Island industrialist.

After 1871, this new Academy served both as Dudley High School and as a "fitting" school for college-bound students. Chapter Five concentrates on the program offered by Mr. Conant's Academy and on life at the Academy in the 1880s. The next chapter follows the Academy's efforts to survive after the death of Conant. And, when local students no longer enrolled in sufficient numbers to keep the school going, the Academy had to be closed in 1909. Its trustees then sought to find a suitable occupant for the buildings on Dudley Hill.

After the Academy came to a halt in 1909, the spirit of Amasa Nichols and its charter of 1819 were carried forward. The Nichols Academy Board of Trustees leased its Dudley Hill property to the Bethel Bible Institute from Spencer, Massachusetts, in 1923. Then, in 1931, it was leased again, this time to Nichols Junior College of Business Administration and Executive Training.

This study is supported by the Nichols College Archives which contains significant resources including Nichols Academy Board of Trustees Meeting minutes, Principals' Reports, catalogues, and accounts of graduations that cover most of the years from 1819 to 1931. It also draws on newspaper accounts, social and educational histories, as well as local histories. It is of interest to educators, local historians, and others concerned about the history of rural Massachusetts, its schools, and all this entails.

The nature and essential spirit of the quest begun by Amasa Nichols and by those who followed him at the Dudley academy, such as industrialist Hezekiah Conant and the Reverend Charles L. Goodell, are part of a complex and enduring heritage that begs to be fully examined. The experience of the American academy in the nineteenth century, as historian James McLachlan insightfully points out, is a "story of the constant interplay of men and ideas, institutions and society."[18] Nichols Academy's history bears this out; its course is fascinating and complex – with numerous bumps along the way.

NICHOLS ACADEMY CAMPUS 1819~1931

Nichols Academy (1819–1873)
In *center* between Universalist Meeting House on *left* and Congregational
Church on *right*. Sketch is from John Warner Barber, *Historical Collections . . .
Massachusetts* (Worcester: Dorr, Howland & Co., 1840), 563.

A folk art watercolor of **Nichols Academy (1819–1863, circa 1839)**
by Tom Menard in 2006. Courtesy Nichols College Archives.

Nichols Academy Campus and Students (1873–1880, circa 1878)

On *left*, the Academy School House (1867–1880), formerly the Universalist Meeting House (1833–1867). On *right*, the new Boarding or Dwelling House (1873–1883). Source: Untitled photograph. Courtesy Nichols College Archives.

Nichols Academy Campus (1882–1883)

From *left*, Conant Library and Observatory, the Academy and Alumni Hall, and Boarding or Dwelling House. Source: Notebook, Hezekiah Conant, Conant Folio, American Antiquarian Society. Courtesy American Antiquarian Society.

Nichols Academy Buildings (1881–1885)
Three buildings financed and constructed by Hezekiah Conant.
Architect was Elbridge Boyden and Son, Worcester, Mass.

Nichols Academy and Alumni Hall (1881)
Constructed in 1881 to replace the Academy School House. Partially
destroyed by hurricane in 1938. Source: *Catalogue . . . Nichols Academy
. . . 1896, Dudley, Mass.*, Insert. Courtesy Nichols College Archives.

Conant Library and Observatory (1882)
Constructed in 1882, this building now is the College Chapel.
Source: *Catalogue . . . Nichols Academy . . . 1896 . . . Dudley, Mass.*,
Insert. Courtesy Nichols College Archives.

Roger Conant Hall (1885)
Built in 1885, this also was called the Dudley Inn. It replaced the
Boarding or Dwelling House. Source: *Catalogue . . . Nichols Academy . . .
1896 . . . Dudley, Mass.*, Insert. Courtesy Nichols College Archives.

9

Academy Campus, Meeting House, and Church (1885–1890)

From *left*, Conant Library and Observatory, Nichols Academy and
Alumni Hall, Conant Hall, Meeting House, and First Congregational Church.
Source: *Catalogue . . . .Nichols Academy . . . 1890, Dudley, Mass.*, back cover.
Courtesy Nichols College Archives.

**Academy Campus, new town school, and
Conant Memorial Church (1893–1931)**

From *left*, Transit building, Conant Library and Observatory, Nichols
Academy and Alumni Hall, Conant Hall, new Dudley Center School,
and First Congregational Church – Conant Memorial. Architect for the
Conant Memorial Church was Francis Wilcox, Providence, Rhode Island.
Source: *Catalogue . . . .Nichols Academy . . . 1896, Dudley, Mass.*, Insert.
Courtesy Nichols College Archives.

Budleigh Hall (circa 1931)
The summer home of Hezekiah Conant was constructed in the 1880s and
purchased by Nichols Academy in 1931 prior to leasing the Academy
campus to Nichols Junior College. Source: Untitled photograph.
Courtesy Nichols College Archives.

CHAPTER 1

THE FIRST ACADEMY:
A DISCORDANT BEGINNING, 1815~1823

After the American Revolution, rural Massachusetts academies emerged in significant numbers. A rapidly expanding commercial and manufacturing economy required basic levels of literacy and education in a society abhorring taxation but seeking opportunity and equality. The educational structure that evolved also reflected its Protestant Christian roots that worked aggressively to promote moral reform and social progress.[1] In turn, each educational experience was part of a special blending of disparate features each seeking to contribute to still forming nineteenth century American ideals.

When Amasa Nichols and his Universalist supporters began the Academy on Dudley Hill, they were hardly alone as academy builders. There were 36 incorporated academies in Massachusetts by 1820.[2] The first of this group was Dummer Academy (now The Governor's Academy) in South Byfield, founded in 1761, followed by Phillips Academy established in Andover in 1780. The number of incorporated Massachusetts academies grew to 68 in 1830; twenty years later, this number reached 135. In neighboring Connecticut, there were 33 academies by 1840.[3] For additional comparison, only 31 free public high schools existed in Massachusetts in 1850. Virtually all were in settled areas.[4]

Founded in 1815 in Dudley, Massachusetts, Nichols Academy was a typically rural academy. It was a private institution that functioned under a state charter, offered a curriculum of classical and English studies, admitted young men and women, charged tuition, and enrolled students from a fairly large geographical area.[5] More specifically, however, Nichols Academy was a product of the wealth and religious zeal of Dudleyite Amasa Nichols who was encouraged by the interest of a small but committed group of New England Universalists. They were supported by the remarkably strong desire of some local leaders to have a secondary school in south central Massachusetts. Its institutional success, however, was not immediately assured. In 1816, a disastrous fire destroyed Nichols' nearly finished first academy building and signaled a difficult start. Fortunately, Amasa Nichols was able to build another structure. The Academy then experienced a lack of funds, internal squabbling, poor preparation, inept management and, in the opinion of some, failure.

A CHALLENGED SOCIETY

Virtually everything changed in America between the American Revolution and the founding of Nichols Academy in 1815.[6] A perceptive observer on Dudley Hill standing next to the Academy would have seen a stream of new Americans moving west and north, some for just a few miles, others headed for New York, Vermont, and the Ohio Valley. Some stayed in the area. They all brought important concerns with them. Nascent feelings of nationalism and independence that surfaced during the revolutionary period now had to be carefully nurtured. Commercial systems had to be rebuilt for national, not empire, purposes. Domestic manufacturing was possible once the new states eliminated British commercial controls, influences, and imperial competition. Industrial development logically was anticipated in areas fortunate to have substantial water power such as Dudley and the surrounding areas in south central Massachusetts touched by the French and Quinebaug Rivers.

Then too, there were general concerns about the redistribution of political power and the effectiveness of the newly adopted national constitution with its federal system. All worried about the potential for taxation and corruption, the unknown dangers of representative government, and the eventual outcome of the democratic experiment. Many in rural societies feared change while acknowledging that the nation's future depended on the education and capabilities of its citizens.

Americans, too, fretted about religion, especially in Massacusetts. Prior to the Revolution, many were starting to rethink the nature and role of religion in their lives. Liberal sects such as the Unitarians and Universalists challenged Calvinist theology by accepting a view of human nature that saw a more benevolent God offering universal salvation to all. Congregationalism and its Calvinist theology had stressed a seemingly vengeful God allowing less opportunity for salvation. At the same time, new questions stemming from classical liberalism and the American Enlightenment looked to reason for answers. Some challenged long-existing religious thinking.[7]

In the context of this changing and, for some, threatening cultural context, education became an even greater factor. America's earliest schools had followed religious themes and purposes. Colonialists in Massachusetts and Connecticut had accepted the right and responsibility of their governments to require towns to establish schools and support the Congregational Church. In the learning environment that resulted, reading focused on religious matters while teaching was permeated by references to the *Hornbook, Primer, Testament,* and the Bible. School systems in colonial Massachusetts communities usually consisted of elementary schools with occasional Latin grammar schools located in distant and larger towns. These Latin grammar schools taught boys aged six to fifteen to read and write in Latin or Greek as a preparation for college and the ministry.[8] Those not involved in these schools attended elementary schools and then used apprenticeship experiences to gain appropriate skills.

By the mid-eighteenth century, America's shifting needs and purposes directly affected its educational development. While changes began before 1775, the Revolution promoted the gradual introduction and expansion of American interests contributing further to the nation's social, cultural, and political growth.[9] By 1790, Latin grammar schools were in decline as rural America grew in population.[10] Consequently, some English grammar schools, more popular in the southern colonies than Latin grammar schools, appeared in New England. These schools featured the aggressive teaching of English, the use of textbooks focusing on the new nation, and the reliance on a broader curriculum including many practical subjects such as those introduced at an academy begun in Philadelphia by Benjamin Franklin in 1751. Franklin summed up his philosophy of educational realism:

> Thus instructed, youth will come out of this school fitted for learning any business, calling or profession, except such wherein languages are required; and though unacquainted with any ancient or foreign tongue, they will be masters of their own, which is of more immediate and general use; and withal will have attained many other valuable accomplishments; the time usually spent in acquiring those languages, often without success, being here employed in laying such a foundation of knowledge and ability as, properly improved, may qualify them to pass through and execute the several offices of civil life, with advantage and reputation to themselves and country.[11]

Franklin's efforts to eliminate the classical theme were not completely successful. In the process, however, he and his supporters contributed to the creation of a practical and distinctively American educational system.

Need, opportunity and an evolving society all figured in the founding of Nichols Academy. Chance alone did not bring an academy to Dudley in south central Massachusetts. Amasa Nichols, owner of the Nichols Cotton Factory in Dudley, played the most important single role in the creation of the Academy that was to bear his name. At the same time, an equally powerful although more subtle force in the Academy's establishment stemmed from a small, but increasingly active group of rural New England Universalists. Their organizational beginnings in central New England in 1785 can be traced to an

Amasa Nichols (1773–1849)
Founder and builder of Nichols Academy in 1819,
a Dudley industrialist and fervent Universalist who served
as secretary of Nichols Academy Board of Trustees (1819–1823).
Photograph by Diane Perry of painting by E.E. Billings from a daguerreotype.
Courtesy Conant Library, Nichols College.

Oxford, Massachusetts, school house in south central Massachusetts. The first Universalist meeting in Dudley, the community next to Oxford, was held several years later in a then "unfinished dwelling house near the Centre. . . ." This probably is now 122 Center Road.[12] Meetings followed that brought scattered Universalists from neighboring towns to Dudley Hill. The idea of a Universalist academy undoubtedly was introduced during these meetings.

Amasa Nichols was born in Thompson, Connecticut, just over the Connecticut state line and south of Dudley on April 2, 1773. His father, David, a Dudley resident before 1792, had been a Universalist and Amasa followed in his footsteps.[13] Amasa married Sally Eaton of Dudley and eventually became a prominent figure in Dudley as a mill owner, merchant, trader, and the little town's post master.[14] Nichols was an energetic and politically involved Dudley citizen, who also was a perennial candidate for election as Dudley's representative to the General Court of the Commonwealth of Massachusetts. In 1812, he was owner of "the cotton factory of Amasa Nichols." Located on the east bank of the French River, this mill was later incorporated as the Dudley Cotton Manufacturing Company.[15]

Between 1803 and 1816, Amasa Nichols acquired at least seventeen different parcels of land, mostly around the Dudley Hill town common, apparently in anticipation of constructing an academy.[16] Nichols began to construct his first academy building next to the town common by 1814 or 1815.[17] The only description of this structure, which referred to Nichols' school as "large and elegant," was provided by a Worcester newspaper after it burned to the ground on April 11, 1816. According to this account:

> the structure [the academy building] contained twelve large rooms for the use of the school and steward, with a spacious chapel above the same, with galleries and a stage for speaking; the whole admirably calculated for exhibitions and the accommodation of such an institution; for beauty and novelty it exceeded any building in this part of the country.[18]

Amasa Nichols' building was to have been finished at a cost of about $10,000 (or nearly $132,600 in 2005 dollars) in 1816.[19] It was ahead of most in terms of cost and design based on the initial descriptions and cost estimates of similar facilities at other academies.[20] Just prior to the fire, a class had begun there under the guidance of Reverend Barton Ballou, a Universalist preacher.[21] After the loss of this building, subscription papers were circulated in the area to help the rebuilding effort, but less than $1,000 was received.[22] There were few supporters in a small community primarily composed of Congregationalists.

Nichols was not discouraged. He sold additional land to pay for a second building, a two-story wooden structure.[23] Within two years he had a shell in place ready for use, although it was in need of painting and further work. This

Rev. Hosea Ballou (1771–1852)
Member of first Nichols Academy Board of Trustees. Influential
Universalist preacher and editor of *Universalist Magazine*.
Courtesy Andover-Harvard Theological Library,
Harvard Divinity School, Harvard University.

new structure reportedly cost an additional $5,000 and probably resembled the design of his first academy building. A "zealous adherent to the tenets of Universalism," Nichols projected its use as a school for Universalists, a meeting house, and eventually as a college for Universalists.[24] While the idea of establishing a college appears somewhat overreaching in 1819, it was consistent with Universalist thoughts and goals pertaining to education.

Although Universalist origins go deep into Europe's past, its American beginnings can be easily traced to the 1780s. Universalists believed in universal salvation directly challenging the Calvinist belief that only a select few – the "elect" – were predestined for Heaven.[25] Universalist sermons and writings were based on the primacy of reason, a respect for human understanding, and the tendency to question tradition.[26] American Universalists, as products of the American Enlightenment, were convinced that reason would lead to greater morality.[27] In a broad sense, they were combining faith and reason to achieve permanent results.

Initially, many rural New England Universalists were former Congregationalists, Baptists, or Methodists who eventually turned to Universalism as a basis for salvation. Their ranks generally were composed of optimistic, but ordinary and poorly educated rural Americans. They were led by a small number of individualistic-minded, liberal, argumentative, and effective debaters who worked to build both a solid body of thought and a dependable religious society. Nonetheless, by 1820 no more than fifty Universalist preachers could be found scattered throughout New England.[28]

Without question, the most outstanding leader of early New England Universalism was Hosea Ballou. Like so many rural Americans, he had little formal education which contributed to his reputation as a man of the people.[29] A self-trained preacher and born debater, his sermons led to an upsurge of liberal thinking in rural New England. He was one of the first Universalists to argue effectively that everyone was to be saved after death. Ballou worked diligently to establish evangelical piety and liberal rationalism as guiding principles for Universalists. During his ministry in Boston, he became a member of the first Nichols Academy Board of Trustees.[30]

Universalists firmly believed that a proper secondary school education was necessary for their children if they were to experience success. Although Ballou and other Universalist preachers had received little formal education themselves, they understood that their children needed an educational background to develop the habits and abilities necessary to understand and follow Christian principles accepted by Universalists. They distrusted established schools of theology believing these schools stamped students with contrary sectarian biases.[31] For Universalists, truth, not religious conversion, was the primary purpose of education. Ultimate truth then led to Universalism.[32]

Since most academies and colleges founded before 1820 had been sponsored or operated by individuals and groups with firm religious connections such as the Baptists, Methodists, and Congregationalists, the children of Universalists had been subject to unwanted sectarian biases in their early educational experiences. At the same time, Universalists did not approve of proselytizing; their educational philosophy called for a learning experience that was capable of challenging formal theology, if necessary. Universalists, one said, only needed "the call of the Spirit, a Bible, and a group of listeners" to promote their form of sectarianism.[33] The Bible was their guide. They claimed that they opposed only those ecclesiastical positions not verified by the Bible or supported by reason.

The idea of a seminary, or academy, was a logical manifestation of their vision. Such a possibility was introduced at a yearly meeting of the New England Universalists at Westmoreland, N.H., in 1814 when a committee was created to consider support for such a proposition.[34] Exactly when Amasa Nichols became directly involved in these deliberations has not been recorded. Given his hopes and enthusiasm, it probably was very early in the process. The convention the following year met in Whitingham, Vermont, and voted to raise $5,000 with the interest to be used to support an unidentified institution. At the convention's next meeting in Charlton, Massachusetts, adjoining Oxford and

Dudley, they reintroduced their efforts to raise money. Further encouragement for a Universalist-supported school was given in 1818 by the convention in Chesterfield, New Hampshire.[35]

THE TRIUMPH OF AMASA NICHOLS

Amasa Nichols completed most of his work on the Academy sometime in 1819. He presented the building to the Academy trustees that summer. The exterior was unpainted; the "victualing" department and dormitory facilities still had to be finished. No matter, the first students or "scholars" enrolled on May 24, 1819. Four of the seven intended to take a twelve-week summer term. This group included two girls: six-year old Sally Nichols and Sally Ellis.[36] Although most students did not enroll before they were twelve years old, a few took a subject or two at an earlier age. Two additional summer terms beginning on July 1st and July 8th added eight and four students respectively. The first formal fall term began in September with an enrollment of 60 "scholars," including eight young women.[37]

That this first group of students began at all was a triumph for Amasa Nichols, but more had to be done. In the brief period between May and December 1819, he assembled a board of trustees, obtained a state charter for Nichols Academy, deeded his building and land to the Academy trustees, had his school accepted by the General Convention of New England Universalists, and helped to write the Academy's constitution and bylaws.

Some academies were supported by gifts. Others had denominational connections and began under ecclesiastical control. Still others were created by private subscriptions.[38] Amasa Nichols' "gift" more than matched most. The act incorporating Nichols Academy was passed by the Massachusetts Senate and House on June 18, 1819, with the Academy's purpose stated as "the promotion of piety and virtue, and for the instruction of youth in such languages, and in such liberal arts and sciences. . . ." This act also listed the members of the Nichols Academy Board of Trustees, described the board's organizational structure and set out a process for the institution's management. Militia General Jonathan Davis of Oxford was to decide the time and place of the board's first meeting.[39]

Nichols Academy was governed by a private, independent board of trustees that received its powers through a state-granted charter. Academy trustees were responsible for overseeing the Academy's organization, administration, and general operation. This included electing their own members and officers, appointing preceptors or principals, and preparing bylaws. The trustees also determined admission policies, protected Academy property, examined students, and inspected the school.[40] Amasa Nichols gave his building and land "containing thirty rods"on Dudley Hill to the Academy trustees on August 7, 1819, for one dollar. The trustees, in return, were required to furnish a "Preceptor for the purpose of instructing youth in said Nichols Academy." If, at any point, the school was not operational for a period of twelve months, the Academy was to be returned to its builder, Amasa Nichols.[41]

These conditions were accepted by the Academy Board of Trustees at its first meeting on August 11, 1819. In line with its charge, the board set tuition at $3 per quarter for English studies and $4 for Latin, Greek, and higher branches of Math. A preceptor was hired for $400 a year with an assistant instructor at an unspecified salary.[42]

When the General Convention of Universalists met in Lebanon, New Hampshire, on September 15, 1819, a Universalist committee reported that "they had succeeded in establishing a Seminary [Academy] of Science in the Town of Dudley, Massachusetts." To what extent this committee had been involved directly in the building's planning and construction is hard to determine. However, according to one historian of Universalism, "each step of the Convention was doubtless <u>incited</u> by Amasa Nichols, Esq., a successful merchant and ardent Universalist of Dudley. . . [underlining is mine]."[43] Members of the Convention voted to "receive the Nichols Academy under their patronage and pledged . . . to use all-proper and reasonable means for the support, respectability and permanence of said institution." One important condition was added: the Convention's support was contingent upon the ability of the Nichols trustees to remain members of the Universalist Convention or to be "in fellowship."[44]

Their agreement did contain one overt promotion of Universalism. It stipulated that "surplus income is to be expended in the free education of young men, of indigent circumstances, but pious and moral habits, designing to enter the gospel ministry."[45] Nichols Academy was the first of twenty academies and at least five colleges, including Tufts College (now Tufts University) and St. Lawrence University, to be supported by Universalists during the nineteenth century.[46]

Nichols Academy's first board of trustees was a most distinguished group. It included four of the most highly respected Universalist leaders in New England. Reverends Hosea Ballou and Paul Dean served the Second and First Universalist Societies, respectively, in Boston. Ballou was the foremost Universalist preacher in New England. Dean, a splendid orator, led the First Universalist Society, which was the largest and most prestigious in the northeast. Reverend Edward Turner at the Charlestown Universalist Society ranked next to Ballou in terms of popularity. Reverend Thomas Jones, the fourth Universalist preacher on the trustees' board, was respected to the extent that he had been called to take over the Gloucester (Massachusetts)

Universalist Society, formerly led by the Reverend John Murray, who was said to be the first important American Universalist.

These Universalist leaders apparently brought four other Universalists from the Boston area to the Academy board. Benjamin Russell was the publisher and editor of the *Columbia Centinel and Massachusetts Federalist* in Boston. Benjamin Gleason was a well-known writer and lecturer. Other Boston-area Universalists who were Nichols trustees were Doctor Abraham R. Thompson and John Kettell from Charlestown.[47] In all, the Boston group of eight trustees composed the board's majority. The other seven trustees, including Amasa Nichols, came from Dudley, Oxford, Charlton, and Southbridge. Time and events quickly demonstrated that it was difficult for the members of this group to work together.

This group's first challenge was to develop the Academy's constitution and bylaws. This was a critical task. A committee composed of Reverends Ballou, Turner and Dean submitted a report in November establishing a Universalist approach to secondary education. It is a significant document that presents Universalist thinking about curriculum structure and purpose as understood by its leading preachers. This curriculum became the Academy's standard for nearly 100 years and, with time, came to represent the general direction of American secondary education in the nineteenth century.[48] This does not suggest that the Universalists turned away from the importance of a Christian base. Article Six of the Nichols *Constitution* notes that the instructor or preceptor had to be a "believer in the Christian Religion." The bylaws and attached regulations also remind readers of their moral mission concluding that: "goodness without knowledge . . . is weak and feeble, yet knowledge without goodness is dangerous. . . ."[49]

Article Six also described a curriculum featuring "English, Latin and Greek Languages, Writing, Arithmetic, Geography, and the art of speaking, also practical Geometry, Logic, and any other of the liberal arts and Sciences or Languages . . ."[50] In effect this curriculum contained a so-called English or practical course intended to co-exist with a classical course for college and university preparation. By not touching on specific denominational tenets, Ballou, Turner and Dean limited the role of sectarian education in the Nichols Academy classroom. This stand was favored by Ballou, who also was the publisher and editor of the *Universalist Magazine*.[51] In effect, Nichols Academy gave the Universalists the opportunity to promote both a rationally-based and morally-oriented secondary institution.

Other Massachusetts academies had taken somewhat different approaches. For instance, Leicester Academy, founded in 1784, had been established by Calvinists and dedicated "to science, literature, and religion." Preceptors at Bridgewater Academy were told to address the school on such issues as God's essential being, "redemptions purchased by Christ," and "future rewards and punishments." The founders of Phillips Andover Academy specified that their master or preceptor should instill in his pupils doctrines of Calvinism such as the depravity of man and the need for atonement.[52] In contrast, Nichols Academy's *Constitution* avoided sectarian references.[53] With the acceptance of its constitution in 1819, the direction of the Academy's curriculum was set.

One important question remains regarding the new institution's beginnings: Why was Dudley selected as its site in the first place? First, the new academy was located in an active although not large area of Universalists – and it was the home of Amasa Nichols. It was to be his academy. In 1785, Universalists from nearby Oxford had organized a meeting of Universalist clergymen later termed the "General Convention of Universalists of the New England States" and then the "United States Convention of Universalists." Between 1785 and 1820, while Universalist societies were organizing in the Boston area, the General Convention still met in Dudley area towns such as Oxford, Charlton, and Sturbridge, as well as in other rural New England locations.[54] While rural, Dudley was a central and logical place for far-ranging society members. Amasa Nichols understood this.

Then too, Reverend Edward Turner, a Universalist member of the Nichols Academy board of trustees, had lived in Sturbridge, attended Leicester Academy in 1792 and 1793, and preached in the Dudley–Charlton area. His supporting role in promoting the Dudley academy cannot be overemphasized. His second wife, Lucy Davis, was the daughter of Levi Davis, a founder of the Oxford Universalist Society. Turner eventually returned to the area in 1827 to lead the Charlton Unitarian Society for several years. Reverend Hosea Ballou also had included the Oxford–Charlton area in his circuit, as had the Reverend Paul Dean. Undoubtedly they had met with Amasa Nichols and the Dudley Universalists on many occasions. Amasa Nichols intended that the Academy's Chapel was to serve local Universalists since a Universalist society had not been formally organized in Dudley.

Dudley offered other advantages for those interested in establishing an academy aside from Amasa Nichols's long connection with the community and the Universalists' interest in rural New England. For one, the population of Dudley had increased from 1,226 in 1810 to 1,651 in 1820, more than a 31 percent increase in ten years. Its population was to reach 2,155 in 1830. Much of this immediate growth was due to the arrival of textile mills along the French River in east Dudley or on Lake Chargoggagoggmanchauggagoggchaubunagungamaugg (also known as Webster Lake). Samuel Slater of Rhode Island had established a manufacturing foothold in south central Massachusetts.[55] Textile manufacturing for a domestic market was about to become a lucrative American industry. Increased commercial activity meant that more people needed the advantages of an education to manage mills and shops and otherwise deal with increasing incomes and the opportunities of commerce. This need was coupled with a growing realization that the emergence of "go-ahead" Americans required a deeper understanding of American society itself. Furthermore, Dudley Hill had been the center of commerce for the area prior to the development of French River mills.

Placement of the Academy on Dudley Hill was important and symbolic. Dudley Hill was the second largest hill in Dudley with a commanding presence that looked into Rhode Island and Connecticut, as well as Massachusetts. The Academy building was located next to the Congregational Church, its Meeting House, and the town common which occupied the top of the Hill. This positioning was not accidental. Their combined presence sent a message of leadership, prominence, and sacrifice (certainly on Amasa Nichols' part as well as others) to rural New Englanders seeking direction. As the Reverend Goodell put it, the Academy stood next to the Church in developing a love of learning among the farmers and the country folk.[56]

Nichols Academy was not without regional competition. Plainfield Academy in Connecticut, eighteen miles away, had been established in 1770. Leicester Academy, fifteen miles to the north in Leicester, Massachusetts, began fourteen years after Plainfield. Amasa Nichols once complained to Reverend Edward Turner about losing two students to the older, larger, and better endowed Leicester Academy.[57] Another academy had been started in nearby Woodstock, Connecticut, ten miles away, in 1802. Early competition between the Nichols and Woodstock Academies is suggested in a history of Woodstock Academy, which refers to the Dudley academy as an "omnipresent" rival.[58]

THE UNIVERSALIST ACADEMY, 1819~1823

Nichols Academy trustees undoubtedly assumed that the first few years were going to be easier after the challenges of starting the institution, writing a constitution, establishing a principal academic building, formalizing support, and enrolling the first students. This was not the case. After some agonizing reflection, one Universalist later said "we builded [sic] a castle in the air and called it a Universalist Academy."[59] Theirs was a noble, if flawed and disorganized effort. The years immediately following 1819 demonstrated the weaknesses of their initial thinking. Poor organization and inadequate financial support resulted in painful and significant adjustments for Nichols Academy and its founder, Amasa Nichols.

At the beginning of 1820, the Nichols Academy Board of Trustees numbered 15 members with eight trustees from the Boston area and seven from around Dudley. The board began its work with Militia General Jonathan Davis from Oxford as presiding officer and Amasa Nichols as secretary. Although no specific statement in the Nichols Academy *Constitution* referred directly to the make-up of the board, all involved understood that this board was to consist entirely of Universalists and those in fellowship in accordance with the vote of the General Convention of Universalists on September 15, 1819.[60] It was not unusual for institutional founders to designate the makeup of their governing boards. For instance, the founders of Phillips Academy in Andover specified that a majority of its trustees reside outside Andover and that this board be composed primarily of laymen rather than ministers.[61]

Financial problems were encountered immediately. More needed to be done although Amasa Nichols had spent $5,000 on his second building after losing $10,000 on the first. The trustees had to complete the upper story of the "second" academy building, which was intended to include boarding accommodations for as many as thirty students, study rooms, and a central section for the academy chapel.[62] Amasa Nichols quickly pushed for additional input from the Universalists.[63] Unfortunately their problem was being exacerbated by a national financial panic in 1819 and a general downturn in the fortunes of American textile manufacturers.

At the first meeting of the Nichols Academy Board of Trustees a request was made that its Universalist members "exert their influence with their friends to procure funds for the school."[64] The next year special agents were appointed to raise funds. A $13 tax was levied on all trustees with delinquent accounts to be turned over to an attorney for collection. Eventually the trustees calculated that $1,000 might be raised in the area.[65] Unfortunately, because income was insufficient to complete necessary repairs and to pay the Academy preceptor, its trustees had no choice but to suspend the school for two quarters in 1822 and 1823. This was not an uncommon practice for financially strapped academies, but it caused a serious rift among board members. Trustee John Brown of Dudley, a strong local Academy supporter and an agent of the Dudley Woolen Manufacturing Company, "threw in" his resignation in apparent anger at the suspension of classes. With time to consider, he returned to the board for the next meeting and also began to teach a class.[66]

An unsettling financial condition was worsened by the Universalists' inability to support the institution. This, in turn, exposed the shaky financial position of Amasa Nichols. That the school did not collapse in late 1822 was a tribute to its remaining trustees. Clearly the Universalists had not been prepared for the challenges and their enthusiasm quickly fell off. Hosea Ballou, the most outstanding Universalist leader in New England, resigned as a Nichols Academy trustee in May 1820, less than a year after the school began.[67] He gave no formal reason for his resignation. Requests to the General Convention of Universalists for additional funds went unanswered despite reminders from the Nichols trustees that "the duty resting on them [the Universalists] that had not yet been performed." Reverend Edward Turner unsuccessfully presented the Academy's position to his fellow Universalists reminding them of ". . . the necessity of immediate measures to support and keep in existence this institution."[68]

Despite favorable reports of Academy activities, a few in Universalist ranks had been skeptical from the beginning. One letter to the *Universalist Magazine* at the end of 1820 reflected growing concerns. The writer, Philo Academicus, a *nom de plume* sometimes used by skeptics, put it this way:

> are the hopes of the permanent establishment of this institution [Nichols Academy] to be raised at a few quarterly examinations as a pleasing prelude to more joyful and lasting realities? Or will they sink and expire . . . It will shortly be seen whether the institution will be supported and made to flourish, or suffered to fall, languish and die.[69]

Uncertainty regarding the Universalists' ability to support Nichols Academy can be sensed in this skepticism. How many Universalists thought like Philo Academicus is difficult to tell. Probably the facts speak for themselves. Three of the Academy trustees who were Universalist preachers or expositors – Reverends Ballou, Turner, and Jones – resigned by 1823 without giving written reasons. So did Universalists John Kettell and Benjamin Russell from Boston and Isaiah Rider from Charlton. While it appears that one new Universalist minister may have joined the board, it also is clear that the Universalist leadership no longer was actively dealing with Academy issues.

One other factor has to be noted regarding the ability of the Universalists to make a meaningful contribution. To gain their Society's full support, the Universalist supporters of Nichols Academy had to work closely together. Crucial here was the long-time friendship between Reverends Ballou and Turner. Their relationship changed, however, when they became embroiled in a significant ecclesiastical controversy beginning about 1818. While all Universalists believed in universal salvation, there was a growing division in their ranks over whether or not God saw the need for some penitential punishment after death and prior to salvation for those committing serious sins.

This schism impacted on the activities of the Nichols Academy trustees. The Reverends Edward Turner and Paul Dean were part of one group, referred to as "restorationists," who believed that limited punishment after death and before final salvation was God's intention. Reverend Ballou, an "ultra-Universalist," thought otherwise and held that any punishment for sins ceased at life's end as all were welcomed immediately into God's kingdom. Unfortunately for the Academy, the debate between Ballou and Turner led to a serious schism in Universalist ranks between 1818 and 1823, as well as a break in their friendship.[70] Their split could not have come at a worse time for Nichols Academy.

Amasa Nichols was experiencing his own financial problems during the first years of the 1820s. This should not be surprising since he had spent approximately $15,000 constructing his buildings. Clearly, Nichols had been depending on Universalist support to complete the second building. Not only did the founder of Nichols Academy have to endure the financial loss related to the Academy buildings, he also was suffering with all small textile manufacturers who found themselves unable to compete with mass-produced cotton goods after 1816.

To offset his significant financial losses, Amasa Nichols continued to sell his land on Dudley Hill and around the Academy. Between 1820 and 1824, he sold eight pieces of property while purchasing only one. Several of his properties adjacent to the town common and the Academy were acquired by Samuel Slater of Pawtucket, Rhode Island. Slater, later referred to as "the father of American Manufactures," had constructed a number of cotton mills in the eastern part of Dudley and in adjacent Oxford South Gore, or what eventually became the town of Webster. At some point, Amasa Nichols apparently offered Slater his land on Dudley Hill. This property was acquired by the Rhode Island industrialist for $7,200, money that probably went to pay some of Amasa Nichols' debts. This sum more than equaled the amount Nichols had paid for the second Academy building.

Slater, now the owner of land adjacent to the Academy, both on the north and south, became a brief but important figure in the early Academy's history.[71] As a consequence of his presence on Dudley Hill, he immediately was made a trustee of the Academy in 1822 although he had no Universalist connections. According to Academy records, Slater did not attend any trustee meetings although he remained a member of the board until his death in 1835. But his support of Amasa Nichols had helped to stabilize the situation around the Academy at a very critical time.

As for Amasa Nichols, not only was he experiencing a personal financial disaster, he had other concerns about his Academy. In one of his few available letters, Nichols wrote to Reverend Edward Turner in May, 1821, about the problems facing the new school. For one, he worried that the number of trustees might fall below the nine members required by the Nichols Academy Charter. This would have resulted in the Charter's loss. He had heard that some trustees were about to resign to avoid the costs of supporting the Academy. Of the trustees, only five had paid their small assessments, again suggesting a weak commitment to the Academy.

Nichols asked Reverend Turner if he thought "whether we have or ever shall have a sum sufficient to warrant perseverance." Amasa Nichols was aware of their fragile situation. If this was not burdensome enough, he also was concerned about enrollment. He commented to Turner that the numbers that summer were satisfactory, about 30 to 40 scholars, but he expected enrollment to fall by 50 percent at the midterm due to a measles outbreak.[72]

By mid-1822, it was obvious that the Universalists could contribute little to the Academy. Amasa Nichols should not have been surprised. He had complained two years before to the Reverend Turner about the lack of support. "It is much to be desired," he wrote to Turner, "that at least some one come up from the center of gravitation [Boston] and express the views. . . . "[73] Apparently this did not happen. By the end of 1823, along with the loss to the board of four Universalist ministers and eight other board members, Nichols resigned his position as board secretary, as well as his membership on the board.

A former Academy student, Holmes Ammidown, believed that Amasa Nichols resigned because the Nichols Academy Board of Trustees had named two local Trinitarian Congregationalists, William Hancock and George A.Tufts, to fill its vacancies. According to Ammidown and others, Nichols argued against this move, but was overruled by remaining trustees. Technically, the Nichols trustees had broken the agreement with the General Convention of New England Universalists to maintain a board of all Universalists or supporters. Reorganization then became the only answer for Nichols Academy. The first Academy had come to an end.[74]

Probably the original agreement on board membership had been untenable in the first place. Nonetheless, by their failure or inability to provide support, the Universalists had contributed to this break. The Academy's inability to pay the Academy preceptor forced the board to suspend the school for two quarters or terms in November 1822.[75] Amasa Nichols resigned then as the direction of Nichols Academy began to change.

While Amasa Nichols railed against the selection of non-Universalists, he was confronted by other issues in 1823. He faced a multitude of calamities, including his own personal bankruptcy. Indeed, evidence of his failing personal financial situation appeared in 1826 and again in 1828 when he was sued for nonpayment of bills and forced to appear at the Court of Common Pleas in Worcester. It appears that he had to pay judgments of $100.23 in one case and $1134.98 in another. Non-compliance would have resulted in his spending time in the county "gaol."[76] At one point, he left Massachusetts for Rhode Island, a commonly used tactic to avoid paying one's debts. There is no record of his return to the area. Nichols may have managed to gather enough property together to satisfy his creditors, but this must have been a sad and humiliating experience.

FAILURE OR SUCCESS?

To conclude that Nichols Academy failed when Amasa Nichols and the Universalists withdrew from the Academy is logical. In fact, however, the Academy was to move beyond 1823 and through the nineteenth century. Institutional barriers that appeared between 1819 and 1823 were overcome by a small but committed group of trustees who came primarily from the Dudley center area.

When the makeup of the Nichols Academy Board of Trustees changed dramatically in 1823, so did the fortunes of the Academy. The Universalist academy came to an end. Local citizens now completely dominated trustee membership. By the end of 1823, seven trustees came from Dudley (this does not count Slater who lived in Rhode Island, although he owned most of the land around the Academy), two each came from Oxford and Charlton, and one from Southbridge. The addresses of two are unknown. Only one, the Reverend Paul Dean, remained from the original group of eight Boston Universalists, but he never attended meetings.

Importantly, most Nichols Academy trustees from Dudley in 1823 were prominent Dudley figures who were either members or former members of Dudley town government. (See Fig. 1.1.) In effect, control of the Academy was now in the hands of local trustees who represented both Universalists and Congregationalists generally living on or near Dudley Hill. They were community leaders as well as members of the town's elite. These commitments to the local community were of great importance in bringing the town and the Academy together. (For a list of Trustees, see Appendix A.)

Not surprisingly, historians of Universalism generally see Nichols Academy as "a failure."[77] After the Nichols experience, Universalist leadership acknowledged that the planning and preparation had been inadequate. Some blamed Amasa Nichols. Another similar venture was not attempted by Universalists until 1831 and the Clinton Liberal Institute, in Clinton, New York. When non-Universalists joined the Nichols Academy Board of Trustees in 1822 and 1823, Universalist control ended, if it actually ever existed. However, although the Universalists had failed in their efforts to operate their first academy, Nichols Academy was not a failure.

As for Amasa Nichols, the confusion that surrounds his resignation still defies full explanation. While many, including Holmes Ammidown, have assumed that he left in protest when non-Universalists appeared on the board, evidence shows Nichols was dealing with his own financial problems as well.[78] Furthermore, he was aware of the flagging support being offered by the Universalists. The fact that the Nichols Academy Board of Trustees meeting minutes do not include any discussion about his resignation suggests his

Fig. 1.1. Nichols Academy Trustees and their Residences, 1823

DUDLEY (with elected town positions)
Jepthah Bacon – Town Assessor, Town Moderator
William Larned – Town Clerk, Selectman
John Brown – Town Moderator, Selectman, State Representative
William Winsor – Selectman
William Hancock – Town Clerk
George A. Tufts – School Examiner
Rev. Abiel Williams – School Examiner

CHARLTON	**PAWTUCKET, R.I.**	**SOUTHBRIDGE**
John Spurr	Samuel Slater	Luther Ammidown
Ira Barton		

OXFORD	**UNKNOWN**	
Jonathan Davis	Rev. Paul Dean	
Jeremiah Kingsbury	Rev. Lewis L. Leonard	

Source: Dudley Town Meeting Minutes, Town of Dudley Meeting Records, 1793–1845, microfilm, FHL, 861113, Genealogical Society of Utah, 1971.

fellow board members did not ask him to reconsider. Amasa Nichols may have believed that the others had failed him.

How much Amasa Nichols' decaying financial situation played in his decision to resign cannot be determined, but it had to have some impact. Less than two years after his resignation, he sued the Nichols Academy Board of Trustees.[79] Perhaps he thought the Academy trustees should have returned the Academy building to him when it officially closed for two terms and was no longer under Universalist control. He had a point. His original agreement with Academy Board of Trustees stated that if the Academy was not operated by an "able Preceptor" for a twelve month period, the Academy was to be returned to its builder. However, nothing further came from his action.[80] Perhaps his personal financial embarrassment left him no choice.

Initial acceptance of the Academy by Dudley Hill residents had not been enthusiastic. Some had been upset and angry about the appearance of the new Academy in the center of Dudley. Writing in 1835, the pastor of the Congregational Church in Dudley and an Academy neighbor, Reverend James H. Francis, referred to Universalism as a "transatlantic heresy" possessing "seeds of error."[81] Francis did not applaud the coming of the Universalist academy. He believed that the Academy was going to provide instruction in "universal religion" and applauded the fact it was "frustrated by the burning of this edifice [the first Nichols Academy building in 1816]." Francis conceded that the building eventually was reconstructed but decided that "it has only, in a limited degree, if at all, subserved, and failed entirely to accomplish, the object which he [Amasa Nichols] intended." Some also may have been upset by the elitist nature of the local trustees who came primarily from the town's center on Dudley Hill.[82]

In many respects, Francis was reflecting what he and others believed. Unfortunately, his intense fervor does not allow him to accept the fact that the Academy was educating Methodists, Congregationalists, and Universalists alike. In contrast, a later Congregational minister, Joshua Bates, D.D., in an "Anniversary Discourse" written nearly twenty years after Reverend Francis and his emotions had cooled, saw the town benefitting from the "advantages of an Academy founded by Amasa Nichols. . . ."[83]

Simply put, the legacy of the General Convention of New England Universalists and Amasa Nichols was not one of failure. Although the Universalists had stopped supporting the Academy by 1823 and had no influence on the school's later operations, Nichols Academy's *Constitution* and general educational philosophy, as developed by Reverends Ballou, Turner, Dean, and probably Amasa Nichols, remained in place. The Universalists may have withdrawn their financial support, but their educational thinking was still embodied in the Academy's purpose.[84]

Importantly for all involved, the broad non-sectarian nature of the Academy's curriculum as created in 1819 was flexible, liberal, and practical. It was consistent with later nineteenth century thinking regarding the nature of secondary education in Massachusetts. For this reason, Universalist families continued to send their children to the Academy throughout the nineteenth century. Over one hundred years after the Academy's inception in 1923, the then president of the Nichols Academy Board of Trustees, the Reverend Charles L. Goodell, a Methodist, pointed to the Academy's continued dedication to the educational spirit originally set forth in its *Constitution* in 1819.[85]

As for Amasa Nichols, there can be little question that he left Dudley a bitter man, probably believing the Universalists had let him down. He died in 1849 at the age of seventy-six in Rhode Island.[86] It is doubtful that he ever returned to Dudley. Nichols Academy could not have been established without his land and his building, not to mention his initiative. The Academy building by itself was a necessary and life-giving contribution. Many early rural academies did not have their own buildings and quickly failed. Academy trustees from the town of Dudley then gave the institution a strong local base. The Academy building of Amasa Nichols eventually was finished and hosted many scholars over the years. Its successors became symbols of his irrevocable and lofty commitment. The Academy's location on Dudley Hill and its educational direction – its place and purpose – had been established by Amasa Nichols and New England Universalists.

CHAPTER 2

THE OLD ACADEMY IN OPERATION, 1823~1860

The educational goal and concerns of the state, the town of Dudley, and the Academy, as well as the nature of Academy students, all must be considered in order to understand the character of Nichols Academy prior to the Civil War. While the Academy functioned independently as a private institution, state educational goals provided much of the context in which it operated. So too did the town of Dudley and the educational products of its elementary schools. Thirty to fifty percent of Academy students came from Dudley's eight or so district elementary schools – one-room schools with eight grades in each. Other students came from throughout Massachusetts, northeastern Connecticut, and northern Rhode Island to what quickly became a highly respected regional academy on Dudley Hill.

THE STATE, THE TOWN, AND THE ACADEMY

Initial experiences of private academies in the Commonwealth of Massachusetts did not alter any basic thinking about the relationship of the state to its internal educational structure. Beginning with the colony's first years, Massachusetts governments had never been far removed from the educational scene. The founders of the Massachusetts Bay Colony determined that all Massachusetts children had to receive a basic education and that Massachusetts towns had to support their schools. Children had to be taught to read the Bible and to understand colonial laws if the colony and its accompanying religious theocracy were to succeed. The principles that all Massachusetts children were required to have a basic education and that towns had to support their schools were introduced by Puritan leadership during the colony's first years.[1] This was a "distinctively" Calvinistic contribution to the new nation and one of great and lasting importance.[2] More specifically, the

Colonial legislature in 1647 ordered every town with 50 households to have a teacher of reading and writing. Towns with 100 or more households had to provide a Latin grammar school. Universal education was understood as vital to the survival of Massachusetts society and the colonial government took full responsibility for its development. This thinking generally was accepted by most New England states, although Rhode Islanders tended to see education as falling into a no-business-of-the-state category.

In practice, colonial and early state laws had uneven outcomes. From the mid-seventeenth century to the end of the eighteenth century, many requirements were ignored locally, although theoretically remaining a central part of the Commonwealth's approach to education. The increasing tendency of new settlers to oppose taxation and a growing disregard of religious-based directives initially contributed to a slow decline in public acceptance of schooling in Massachusetts. However, the trauma of the American Revolution and the general insecurity caused by independence alerted many to the fact that the new nation's survival was dependent on the wisdom and productivity of its people. As rural communities grew in population and importance, towns relied more and more on their local district schools resulting in the need for additional qualified teachers. This caused an expanding educational base, more public involvement, and the emergence of academies.

Massachusetts law originally sanctioned the legitimacy of local school districts in 1789. This gave independent governmental power to specified local districts as they charted elementary school development within Commonwealth towns.[3] Most one-room district schools were run by voters in their school districts. The town of Dudley had eight such districts at one early point. Massachusetts law in 1789 also required that towns with 50 to 100 families support an English grammar school. This school was to be open six months a year and to teach reading, writing, orthography, the English language, arithmetic, and decent behavior. If a town had 100 families or more, it had to make elementary schooling available for a twelve-month period for its young citizens.[4] While few communities followed these laws to the letter, models for a state educational system were being put in place.

Private academies were not ignored in this early educational development process. In fact, public and private education functioned briefly as a partnership.[5] Consistent with the state's commitment to assist in the overall development of a state-wide educational system, a Massachusetts legislative committee chaired by Nathan Dane in 1797 recommended that the Commonwealth make land grants of one-half a township in its Maine district to eligible academies. These grants required that academies demonstrate financial security by having $3,000 on hand. Since these funds were not available in Nichols Academy's case, the Nichols board of trustees promoted a local subscription effort that eventually resulted in subscriptions totaling $2,101. The school later presented this fund raising effort as evidence of fiscal responsibility and received a Maine land grant worth about $2,500. This made Nichols Academy's survival possible.[6]

State interest in directing Massachusetts education was reemphasized in an 1827 law that most agree was the beginning of the public high school movement in the United States.[7] This law required that every town having over 500 families had to teach United States history, bookkeeping, algebra, geometry, and surveying. If a town had 4,000 or more inhabitants, instruction in Greek, Latin, history, rhetoric, and logic also had to be offered. In effect, the seeds of the American public high school system were being planted just as the Academy was about to mature. In the long run, the Massachusetts approach to public education became the primary model for much of American education.

Academies, as well as local school systems, were affected by the 1827 law. Some academies felt threatened and immediately joined with beginning high schools in communities such as Gloucester, Marblehead, and Nantucket. In Framingham, the local academy gave its property to the high school one day and former academy students went to the new high school in the same building the next day.[8] Nonetheless, in the early 1800s, most people saw Massachusetts academies, such as Nichols, as parts of an emerging, but still vaguely defined educational system.

More directly, the Act of 1827 that required communities to provide secondary school education at the taxpayers' expense pushed Nichols Academy and the town of Dudley into thoughtful discussions.[9] At a February 1828 meeting, the Nichols trustees voted to propose to the town that it send its students to the Academy at a minimal cost to the local taxpayers. A receptive town committee then recommended that the town pay a yearly fee of $250 to cover all Dudley pupils qualified to study at Nichols Academy.[10] The Academy agreed beginning with the 1828 spring term.[11]

In order to attend the Academy, candidates for admission were required to pass an examination supervised by an examining committee made up of four town and five Academy representatives. Thanks to its Universalist design, the small rural community of Dudley already had a broad, carefully crafted curriculum available at the Academy that fit general state guidelines for high schools. At that moment, the town added a vital educational component to its existing district school system and the Academy acquired a constant flow of local students virtually assuring uninterrupted operation – as long as the agreement lasted. Surprisingly, it remained in effect only one year.

THE "SCHOLARS"

"Scholars" entered the Academy even before Amasa Nichols' school had received its charter and Universalist support. For its first year beginning in May 1819 and ending in June 1820, Nichols Academy enrolled a total of 144 registrants over the four terms although only a small number were interested in attending for more than one term. Consistent with a long-existing pattern of attendance in Dudley elementary schools, 70 percent of the scholars attended only one term. Thirty-six, or 25 percent, of the first year's group were women. Between May 1819 and May 1827, 1,025 scholars registered, or an average of 128 a year; this included 211 young women, or approximately 24 a year.[12] Between 1822 and 1828, an average of 16 scholars a year boarded in the Academy building's small rooms.[13] The others, perhaps more than 100 in a year, boarded in private homes on Dudley Hill.

Nichols Academy's first scholars, a few younger than 12 years old, came from locations in central Massachusetts extending into northeastern Connecticut and northwestern Rhode Island. Amasa Nichols identified his first group of scholars as coming mostly from Grafton (to the northeast of Dudley), apparently due to the influence of a clergyman there, and from Shrewsbury, Barre, Western (now Warren), Brookfield, and Sturbridge in Massachusetts, and Pomfret and Thompson in Connecticut, as well as from Dudley. Amasa Nichols referred approvingly to several who were the sons of "literary gentlemen" and preparing for college at Nichols Academy.[14] In the 1826–1827 year, Academy records show 96 students in attendance from 13 central New England communities and three states.[15] In addressing the question about which part of the year was favored by young "scholars," Amasa Nichols once responded "you know Country people want their sons in summer to work, Cities and towns do not."[16]

Several revealing statistics come from enrollment records related to the Academy-Dudley agreement in 1828. Not surprisingly, enrollment in one year increased from 85 scholars in the 1826–1827 year to 102 in 1827–1828. The number of Dudley students enrolled at the Academy increased from 39 percent (37 out of 95) in 1826–1827 to 42 percent (51 out of 121) in 1827–1828. Young women made up nearly 60 percent of the 1827–1828 Dudley total. In all, fifteen towns, including two in Rhode Island and three in Connecticut, were represented in the student body that year.[17]

At the same time that the town of Dudley and the Academy established an educational partnership, Nichols Academy also created a "female school." This required that the trustees hire an instructor or preceptress for a department of female education although this move was delayed into 1829.[18] The admission of young women to New England academies prior to 1820 was not new. This was done at many New England academies such as Greenfield Hill in

Connecticut and Monson Academy and Amherst Academy in Massachusetts, among others. But Nichols Academy made it possible for many young women in south central Massachusetts, and somewhat beyond, to receive a secondary school education previously not available.

Operating the Academy did become easier with time. For instance, hiring a preceptor for a two-year period could be better organized as more academies emerged. A steward to oversee boarding facilities also was hired. The trustees regularly rented an additional apartment in the Academy building for added income. By 1835, the size of the enrollment began to reflect the school's increasing popularity. Scholars in 1835 came from 20 towns as far away as Boston to the east and Troy and Poughkeepsie in New York to the west joining other Nichols "scholars," including 35 from Dudley. Fifty-one, or 45 percent, out of 114 students, were women. Of the Dudley scholars who were no longer financially supported by the town, 20 or 57 percent were women. Aside from the Dudley group, at least ten students came from each of nearby communities of Southbridge, Woodstock in Connecticut, Webster (the town created from Oxford and Dudley in 1832), and Charlton.[19]

Academy leaders made every effort to develop a proper and controlled learning environment. This included instructions for townspeople who were boarding students. Scholars were provided with a structured day – from sun-up to sun-down – and beyond. To start the day off right, the Academy's board decided that scholars should study one hour in the morning beginning at six o'clock from April to June. They also were to study one half hour in the evening to begin no later than eight o'clock. During the summer term, studying began at 5:30 in the morning for one and one-half hours. Times of rising did vary depending on the scholar's age, with consideration given to younger scholars. Those who were 14 years or older rose at five or sunrise; those under 14 could get up at six from March to September. From September to March, they were up at six and seven, respectively.[20]

Abigail Ormsbee from Dudley and a Nichols "scholar" in 1839, later recalled these regulations and filled in some of the details in her schedule. After rising one-half hour before sunrise, she cleaned her teeth, brushed her hair, and dressed for the day. After breakfast, she made her bed, put her room in order, and arranged her wardrobe "with care." Further reminders for her day, which she noted on her schedule, included not eating between meals and retiring by ten o'clock.[21]

Daily class schedules reflected a similar reliance on structure and community participation. Many activities involved the entire student body acting as a group. For instance, the first half hour of each day featured a general exercise in which "all pupils" were involved. Two mornings each week, the student body focused on the "elementary sounds of the English language, exercising the organs in articulating difficult combinations of consonants, and considering familiar criticisms of the common errors of punctuation." This must have been an interesting way to begin the day. Two other mornings consisted of reading selected passages with the intention of breaking "bad habits" and to "render the pupils forcible, expressive and natural readers." Parts of two mornings were allotted to exercises in composition and in "connection with familiar lectures in style." Additionally, lectures and programs also were given on "elocution" and might include philosophical topics illustrated by experiments. Presumably the various other subjects were taken at available intervals throughout the day. While the value of this community educational approach is difficult to assess nearly two hundred years later, it must have had a powerful impact on those fully committed to acquiring an education.[22]

To assure that student meals were wholesome, daily menus for Academy students boarding at the Academy were designed by trustees. They were somewhat nutritious, but not much more. Breakfast consisted of coffee, warm wheat bread and butter. Noon dinners, six days a week, featured some kind of meat with vegetables and bread and butter. On Sunday, this included bread and butter, or pie and cheese if convenient for the steward, and water to drink. Suppers featured tea, with bread, butter and cheese. And, perhaps twice a week, pie, gingerbread, or cake was served. This rather spartan fare was included in the $1.50 per week room cost. Those who boarded in the village on Dudley Hill either ate with Dudley families or managed on their own with food brought from home.[23]

Between 1819 and 1846, Nichols Academy offered four eleven-week terms a year including one in the summer. The term structure changed in 1846 to three twelve-week terms. Scholars had the option of attending one, two or three terms as well as a summer term, at least until 1846. A sampling of data for the 1826-1827 fall-winter-spring terms shows that of 79 individual enrollees, 62, or 77 percent, went one term that year, 14 went two terms, and three went for three terms.[24] A similar sampling of a like three-term period in 1850–1851 finds that the individual scholars continued to follow the same pattern. Sixty-three, or 78 percent, stayed only one term while 16 remained two terms and two for three terms in the 1850–1851 school year.[25] Ten years later, out of the 159 Nichols Academy students enrolled, 114, or 72 percent, went only one term, 31 went for two terms and 14 enrolled for all three terms.[26] Little had changed. Although some enrollment periods present somewhat different data, there is no question that virtually three out of four scholars in these pre-Civil War years attended Nichols Academy for only one term during the year. This is essentially what they had done in elementary school.

How beneficial could a one-term-a-year education have been? Did these one-termers work on the family farm the rest of the time? Certainly many did. However, a great many were serving apprenticeships in local mills and shoe shops or working in other commercial enterprises. Those on the farm were working with land: farming, measuring, surveying, selling and buying. Members of this group could return to the Academy, as many did, to take subjects such as bookkeeping, geometry, practical mathematics, mensuration, and trigonometry. What appeared during the pre-Civil War period was a subtle but sensible coordination of work and academic subjects that generally has not been appreciated. For instance, the personnel records of Dudley men who later enlisted in the Civil War reveal at least thirty-three different occupations led by farmers, shoe workers and carpenters.[27] The full effect of this nineteenth century "cooperative" educational pattern has yet to be studied, but it clearly was present in antebellum rural Massachusetts.

Despite what appears to be a successful institution in the 1840s, enrollment at Nichols Academy remained static. In the 1845–1846 academic year, 48 men and 43 women or 91 scholars enrolled; in 1850–1851 year, 47 men and 55 women made up a student body of 102.[28] By way of comparison, Leicester Academy registered 225 scholars over four terms the next year.[29] Stability at the Dudley academy did allow its trustees the chance to focus on categorizing their responsibilities. By 1852, they were aiming to publish a catalog annually, hire more experienced preceptors, work with a steward, audit accounts, complete repairs to the Academy building, and review the Academy's *Constitution*, although they made few changes. Their discussions did not focus directly on the future. It is quite probable that the Academy trustees believed the state was going to assist, if necessary.

"THERE SHALL BE TAUGHT"[30]

Nichols Academy trustees continued to be active after the early and difficult years. Soon after starting in 1823, the board was confronted with the challenge of keeping the school open when it failed to receive expected support from the General Convention of Universalists. Trustees John Brown and William Winsor actually filled in and taught some subjects in the Academy building. Then the reorganized trustee board immediately agreed to hire a new preceptor. Under the 1819 Nichols–Universalist agreement, the preceptor's salary was to have been paid by the Universalists. In 1823, the board turned over all tuition income to its Academy preceptor.[31] This was the only income available.

Within a few years, the trustees set out to finish the "academy" building begun ten years before by Amasa Nichols. Initially a building committee decided the structure was "fast decaying and in very bad condition."[32] Certainly they were in a better position to deal with their problem although they still could not complete the entire building. Fortunately, the subscription drive begun in 1823 had brought in $2,101.[33] When added to the value of the Maine grant land from the Commonwealth of Massachusetts, a total of $4,250

Fig. 2.1. Notice of Nichols Academy, 1828

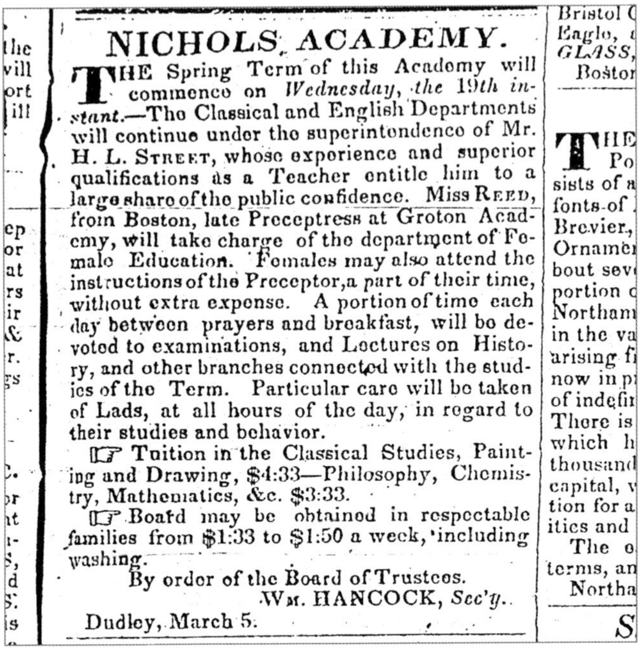

NICHOLS ACADEMY.

THE Spring Term of this Academy will commence on *Wednesday, the 19th instant.*—The Classical and English Departments will continue under the superintendence of Mr. H. L. STREET, whose experience and superior qualifications as a Teacher entitle him to a large share of the public confidence. Miss REED, from Boston, late Preceptress at Groton Academy, will take charge of the department of Female Education. Females may also attend the instructions of the Preceptor, a part of their time, without extra expense. A portion of time each day between prayers and breakfast, will be devoted to examinations, and Lectures on History, and other branches connected with the studies of the Term. Particular care will be taken of Lads, at all hours of the day, in regard to their studies and behavior.

☞ Tuition in the Classical Studies, Painting and Drawing, $4:33—Philosophy, Chemistry, Mathematics, &c. $3:33.

☞ Board may be obtained in respectable families from $1:33 to $1:50 a week, including washing.

By order of the Board of Trustees.
WM. HANCOCK, Sec'y.

Dudley, March 5.

Source: *Massachusetts Spy*, March 5, 1828. Courtesy American Antiquarian Society.

became available for the Academy building and boarding facilities. A trustee committee of William Hancock and the ubiquitous Dudleyite, John Brown, recommended "mending" or replacing windows above the lower story or cellar, finishing the northeast room for the use of the "female school," and making repairs to the chapel at a cost of three hundred to five hundred dollars.[34] In 1828, an increasing sense of success led the trustees to publish notices of the Academy's availability in newspapers as far away as Boston.[35] (See Fig. 2.1.) They had come a long way since January 1823.

When Amasa Nichols and the Universalists leaders discussed the curriculum of the Academy in 1819, they understood this was a foremost and crucial matter. It had to be devoid of any sectarian influence. Consequently, they agreed that Nichols Academy was to offer a program including the following subjects: "the English, Latin and Greek Languages, Writing, Arithmetic, Geography, and the art of speaking, also practical Geometry, Logic, and any other of the liberal arts and Sciences or Languages, as opportunity may hereafter admit. . . ."[36] As an Academy catalogue later put it, this curriculum was "free from the incalculations of any sectarian principles of religion."[37] This was critical. The Academy remained committed to this non-sectarian curriculum despite its break with the General Convention of New

England Universalists. This commitment resulted in the selection of certain courses and general course alignment. There were no theology courses. Their thinking was steadfast; a liberal education was intended to expand ideas, improve understanding, and strengthen morality.[38] Interestingly, the nature of student academic work at this time usually is best described as "book learning" and included whatever lent itself to being written down, memorized, and recited. Not included in the Academy's offering were subjects of a vocational nature where necessary skills were acquired through actual learning experiences best achieved through apprenticeships.[39]

Practical exigencies made it important that courses be appealing and useful. This led to the Academy's continued support and promotion of two programs or branches: the Classical course and the English course. This approach had been implemented by academies as early as the 1750s. The Nichols curriculum featured one program (Latin and Greek) for college and seminary bound students and one of a practical nature (English).[40] For a time, "scholars" younger than twelve years of age were admitted to the Academy paying two dollars for the basic program, presumably the English offering, but could take only two subjects. This curriculum structure, although not its fees, was to remain with the Academy for nearly a century.

While the Nichols Academy curriculum initially had been intended to serve a broad community of Universalists, it also offered a basic secondary school education for everyone in the area. Over the first half of the nineteenth century, 30 to 40 percent of Academy students were sons and daughters of Dudley families. They were products of a rural Dudley school system that was subject to the dictates of the Commonwealth of Massachusetts and the ideas of numerous local Dudley school districts. Most Nichols "scholars" from outside Dudley were from other similar Massachusetts and Connecticut communities and probably had like backgrounds. Some undoubtedly were Universalists.

Dudley, as was the case with other rural Massachusetts communities, had constructed its elementary school system around its district schools. Residents of local districts ran their own schools and decided the nature and actual location of these schools within the designated districts. They also selected their teachers, created their budgets (generally limited by the town of Dudley to $100), and had input into course selection. Prior to 1832, eight district elementary schools were located in the various parts of Dudley to be attended by "scholars" in that district. By comparison, the somewhat larger Sturbridge community to the west had 13 school districts.[41] The voters of Dudley in these early years traditionally voted $800 for school expenses to be divided equally between the districts. These schools generally were open for three months in the summer and a similar period in the winter.[42] The common school curriculum, according to one historian, "was so brief that it could be covered by a bright boy in a year or two, and so narrow that it could be contained in one small volume."[43] Children between the ages of five to fifteen years were eligible to attend district elementary schools in Dudley.

Levels of learning in district elementary schools undoubtedly varied from year to year and from teacher to teacher. Many teachers received their educational backgrounds in local academies such as Nichols Academy. Generally a child's earliest elementary school training began with letters and syllables, reading, writing, spelling, numbers, elementary language, and good behavior. The older children usually took advanced reading, advanced spelling, word analysis, penmanship, arithmetic, geography, grammar, U. S. History, and manners and morals. Girls might receive some additional instruction in sewing and darning.[44] Once the elementary school program had been completed, the "scholar" could go on to a secondary school such as an academy or a high school, if available.

Dudley's agreement to send its students to the Academy in 1828 is important for historians since it also identified the level of preparation required for Dudley's scholars (and others as well) to enter the Academy. Dudley representatives and Nichols trustees agreed that applicants had to understand the necessary parts of the spelling book, the sounds of consonants, punctuate properly, read with a "good degree of accuracy," spell with skill, and understand English grammar. In addition, young men had to be familiar with arithmetic: addition, subtraction, multiplication, division, and reduction. Young women were excluded from this latter requirement. Importantly, this helps to distinguish between elementary and secondary school requirements in one rural town in 1828.[45]

Surprisingly, when the town of Dudley was given the opportunity to extend its arrangement with the Academy, the town meeting the next year "decided in the negative" without leaving a statement in the record as to their reasoning.[46] To what extent their decision might have been influenced by the fact the Academy was privately controlled cannot be determined. Certainly the somewhat elitist nature of the Academy trustees may have been an issue. Most trustees lived on or near Dudley Hill or Dudley Center and it is probable that a large percentage of Academy students came from the Hill as well. There also is no question that some in Dudley had a high regard and enthusiasm for free public elementary education as evidenced by their commitments to maintaining and operating their district schools. But many had sent their children to the Academy at their own expense before the formal agreement between the town and the Academy in 1828 so it is hard to imagine their opposition to a later agreement. Too, the cost to the town, as small as it seemed, may have been a factor since not everyone believed that all children should have schooling beyond the elementary level. But the Academy continued to grow despite the fact that the first agreement between the Academy and the town ended in 1829. It was not to be the last such agreement.

As the desire for more extensive educational opportunities had increased, academies such as Nichols had replaced some Latin grammar schools by offering classical courses. At Nichols Academy in 1834, of 74 "scholars," seven can be found studying Latin and three Greek. The next year ten males and one female were listed as Latin scholars while five males and one female were enrolled as Greek scholars. Two young men were both Latin and Greek scholars.[47] Generally the Academy's classical course took four years although this too was flexible. The determining factor was the student's ability to be admitted to college. This usually was achieved through an entrance exam at the college or university involved. In some instances different arrangements might be made with individual colleges. For instance, Leicester Academy in Leicester, Massachusetts, complained that some of its students were leaving for college after only three years against the wishes and without the support of the Academy.[48] For much of the nineteenth century, the line between academies and colleges was unclear. Many academies did have ties with some institutions, but Nichols Academy records do not identify any direct affiliations.[49]

More practical than the Classical program was the Academy's common English course that covered a wider range of subjects. Generally a much greater percentage of Nichols Academy students took this course. Essentially it was composed of all subjects in English and included classes in reading, grammar and spelling. The English course also included geography, ancient and modern history, history of the United States, sciences, mathematics, logic, philosophy, bookkeeping, and surveying, among others.[50] Academies along the coast frequently added navigation and some foreign languages to their lists of practical subjects.

The intention and strength of the common English course was to build individual communicative skills as well as to sharpen individual perceptions of their roles as American citizens. In 1834, aside from the ten students committed to Latin and Greek, eight other Nichols scholars were studying algebra, four were in chemistry, five astronomy, nine natural philosophy, three rhetoric, and one logic. This was an impressive range of selections. French and Italian were introduced into the curriculum in the late 1840s.[51] Students who performed successfully in the "Common English" program were encouraged to take advanced subjects.[52] Interestingly, the study of English generally focused first on grammar, then composition, and, finally, literature. Primary goals were to write and communicate effectively. In 1845, the Academy pointed to the fact its students were offered a "thorough, systematic, and practical education."[53]

Without much advance notice, a new Academy program emerged in the late 1820s that demonstrated the sensitivity of academies to societal needs. As elementary schools expanded in number and importance, educational leaders recognized the need for teacher training programs. With new books about teaching by Samuel Reed Hall (*Lectures on School-Keeping*) and Jacob Abbott (*The Teacher*), soon to be available, at least 18 New England academies were beginning to educate prospective teachers.[54] In 1834, 16 Nichols Academy students (out of 74 that year) indicated interest in becoming a teacher. At first, the Dudley Academy's program only offered potential teachers advanced instruction in subjects normally found in the academy curriculum. Knowledge of one's subject matter was seen as the primary requirement for prospective teachers. Initially there was little focus on methods of teaching. This changed by 1846, as noted by the Nichols Academy catalogue, which referred to "lectures being on subjects" that were connected with the art of teaching and "calculated for the business of Instructors."[55] Fourteen years later the Academy reported that a large number of "both sexes" intended to become teachers.[56]

Interest of academies in teaching programs was important to the larger educational picture as well. The Academy's commitment to educate future teachers resulted in upgrading elementary school education by contributing to a better educational base and generally building a more favorable mind set regarding the development of education in rural areas. Nichols Academy became a primary source of elementary school teachers for the region without initially making a great effort to do so. Eventually, Massachusetts created a state supported normal school system, but the Academy trained teachers into the 1870s. According to the assessment of one historian of education, the antebellum years were "probably the most significant ones in the whole history" of the teaching profession.[57] The Nichols Academy experience further documents a building interest in teaching and local education.

New instructional methodology and technology also was being introduced throughout this period. Seemingly minor by modern program standards, these adjustments and improvements played important roles in improving the educational environment. Some academies employed a system generally associated with Joseph Lancaster, an English Quaker schoolmaster, that featured large classes, untrained assistants or monitors who were sometimes older students, and a recitational approach. The teacher used the textbook to give students information which was then recited word for word until correct. This system was economical, expedient, easily followed, unimaginative, and mechanical.[58] It is probable that Nichols students experienced attempts by preceptors to utilize any number of approaches, although the system of memorization did not disappear quickly.

Textbooks were difficult for Academy students to procure as late as the 1840s. Some students had their own books, either from an older sibling or a former student. Some preceptors left their books outside their suites for students' use. Such an informal "library" was all that was available to Nichols

Fig. 2.2. Nichols Academy Textbooks, 1835 and 1850–1851

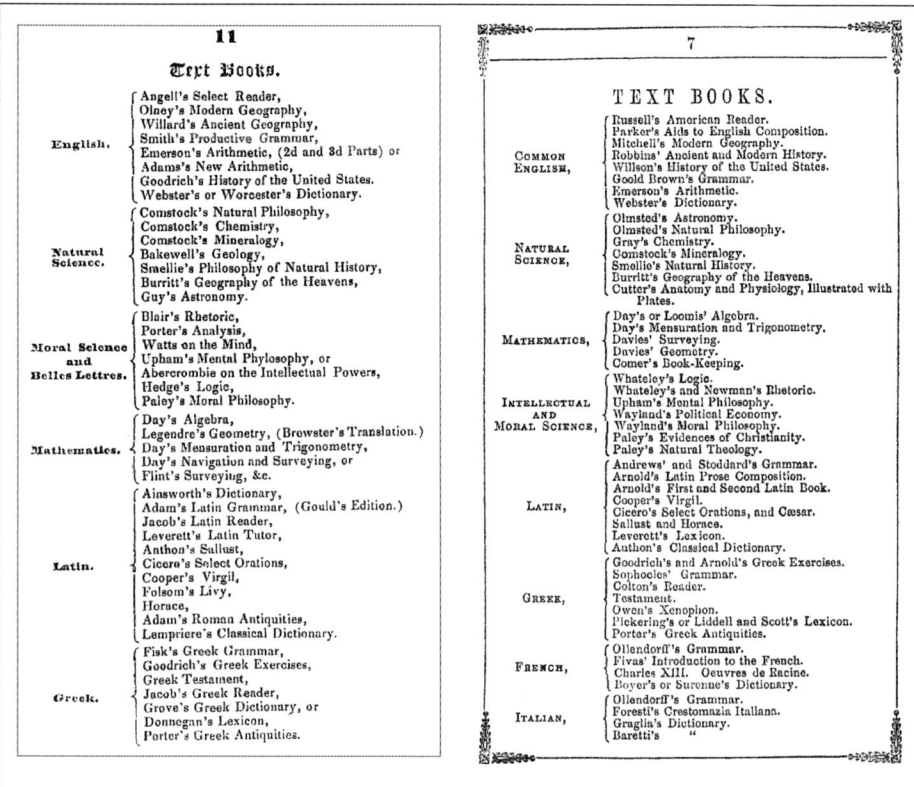

Sources: *Catalogue . . . Nichols Academy . . . 1835, Dudley, Mass.* (Worcester, Mass.: Moses W. Grout, 1835) 11, NCA; *Catalogue . . . Nichols Academy, Dudley, Mass., 1850–1851* (Worcester, Mass.: Henry J. Howland, n.d.) 7, NCA.

students until 1882. On one occasion, and with more than a slight hint of envy, Amasa Nichols reported to his trustees in 1821 that Leicester Academy had a library, but this was the exception.[59] Academy catalogues usually contained a list of books used in various subjects making it easier for students to plan for their subjects and to get textbooks in advance. (See Fig. 2.2.) Fortunately, Americans began to publish books for the "academy" market by the 1820s. For instance, Noah Webster sought to standardize American spelling and punctuation in his books. Jedidiah Morse from nearby Woodstock in Connecticut was helping to introduce United States geography. Another, Elijah Burrett, who taught at Sanderson Academy in Ashfield, Massachusetts, published his popular *Geography of the Heavens* for astronomy classes.[60] These texts were important for awakening American children to a vital national identity.[61] A comparison of textbooks used at Nichols in 1850 with those used earlier in 1835 suggests the expansion and adjusting tendency of the curriculum as well as a continued adherence to the twin themes of the classical and the practical.

A student's daily performance could be a trying experience. Even the simple act of obtaining writing utensils was time consuming. It probably took as long to learn how to mend quill pens as it took to develop good penmanship. In fact, penmanship was taught at many academies, including Nichols, although it might be offered early in the morning or late at night when time was available. Individual slates with wooden frames also began to appear in the 1820s as did lead pencils, both necessary for studies.[62] Philosophical apparatus (physics was referred to as natural philosophy), seemingly a beginning for science courses, did not appear at Nichols until 1845, and then only after the trustees were pressured to buy some equipment by an incoming preceptor.

"REGULARITY IN THE BEHAVIOR OF SCHOLARS"[63]

Rules for the conduct of Academy scholars were spelled out in the Academy's *Constitution*. Initial regulations reflected concerns about boarding arrangements, the need to protect and respect the Sabbath, and the importance of eliminating disorderly behavior as well as avoiding habits not conducive to a proper moral environment. Of great importance in this educational process were the heads of households where "scholars" boarded. In effect, these Dudley home owners were partners of the Academy. Even after the Academy building was ready for boarders, other boarding locations on Dudley Hill remained a integral part of the learning community.

In a formal sense, the Nichols Academy's *Constitution* provided the following "Regulations" for the old Academy and, indirectly, for the entire village. These regulations as stated in the *Constitution* need to be repeated:

> The Trustees of Nichols Academy, taking into consideration the great importance of regularity in the behavior of scholars out of the academy as well as when under the immediate eye of their Instructors, and especially in the families in which they board as disorderly behavior and bad habits, indulged there, will defeat every endeavor to form their minds, morals and manners, and considering the necessity of heads of families seconding the views of the Founders, Trustees and Instructors; have instituted the following regulation, which they hope will be punctually observed, and that the trouble of boarding will be thereby lessened, while the true interest of the scholars is promoted.

I.

It is expected, that no scholar be allowed to be from home after nine o'clock in the evening.

II.

It is expected, that heads of families will use their best endeavors, when necessary, to make scholars, while boarding with them, observe such hours as the Instructor shall from time to time direct.

From the first of April to the Spring vacation, the Scholars are to study half an hour in the evening, and one hour in the morning, the evening study to begin at eight o'clock, and the morning study at six o'clock. During the summer term, there must be one and a half hours study in the morning commencing at half past five o'clock. From the beginning of the Fall term to the first of April there must be one and a half hours study in the Evening, commencing at seven o'clock. From the 21st of March to the 21st of September, those scholars who are above fourteen years of age are to rise at 5 o'clock or as soon as the sun rise and those, who are under fourteen at 6 o'clock; and from the 21st of September to the 21st of March must rise as soon after 6 o'clock as the sun shall rise; but they shall never lie after 7 o'clock.

III.

It is expected, that every scholar when health and weather permit, be required to attend public worship, seasonably and constantly, on the Sabbath; and on other parts of the day to be observant of the rules of propensity and decorum.

IV.

It is expected, that all the fighting, striking, quarreling and opprobrious language among scholars be strictly forbidden and utterly discontinued by those who receive boarders.

V.

It is also expected, that all profane and obscene language, and card playing will be prohibited and guarded against among boarders. But if any scholar is guilty of either of these, it is expected that the husband or head of the family acquaint the instructor therewith.

VI.

It is required, that the boarders retire to rest at reasonable hours; and in the morning be in readiness to attend the duties of the Academy.

VII.

When any scholar is going from his lodgings in the Evenings, he is required to inform one of the heads of the family, of the place to which he is going, and all the scholars are forbidden to go into bad company, or to any public house, unless with a parent or guardian or with permission of the Instructor.

VIII.

As it is the wish of the Trustees not to impose any restrictions or regulations, whereby the difficulties of boarding may be increased, but on the contrary to lessen and to remove them; so if it be found by experience, that any of these regulations are either grievous or impractical it is expected that information will be immediately given to the Instructor who will lay the same before the Trustees as soon as may be, that the subject may be examined and such alterations made, as to them may appear necessary.[64]

With experience and a better understanding of their scholars, the Academy trustees made some changes in 1835 for the sake of brevity and effectiveness. Of six rewritten rules, three dealt with individual conduct noting the need for "due respect" and the belief that "scholars" had to "observe propriety of deportment" in their relations with each other. Profane language, card playing, and other games of chance were forbidden suggesting that these activities continued to be problems. The new rules gave greater power to the preceptor to determine the times and hours of study. Regulations regarding attendance at public worship were not changed significantly, although the trustees did add that parents and guardians, as well as the preceptor, could excuse the scholars from attendance. In short, experience had dictated a need for tighter reins in some areas and occasional flexibility in others.[65]

PRECEPTORS

Day-to-day conduct of the school was the responsibility of a preceptor or principal. Not surprisingly, there were few specific guidelines for staffing a new academy that periodically experienced fluctuating attendance and suffered from insufficient housing, inadequate income, and a lack of textbooks. Generally preceptors were given full rein over the academic program and daily operations. They usually taught classical subjects with an assistant or two covering the practical course. A steward may have been hired to manage the boarding facilities, although, on occasion, an aggressive preceptor performed the steward's duties as well.

Since preceptors came from various institutions of higher learning, they introduced their different pedagogical and personal approaches and reflected varied educational backgrounds throughout many northeastern academies and areas, including Nichols and Dudley. This is extremely important, but frequently overlooked. As hectic and ineffective as some of their activities appear, the process of education was crucial as it became both the maker of new citizens and the builder of a new nation.

Twenty-five preceptors served the Academy over its first forty years. (See Appendix B.) This number was not out of line with the experiences of other small rural academies.[66] Candidates for preceptor's positions, usually recent college graduates interested in a one or two year appointment, were interviewed first by a trustee committee. Apparently this was a standard arrangement. Initially, preceptors were paid $400 to $500, sometimes less. Comments suggest that these arrangements were negotiated on conditions of the moment, and frequently based on anticipated tuition income. Most preceptors stayed no more than two years in accordance with the usual practice. Those who did not like conditions might opt to get out of their contracts after one year. Clearly there was much difficulty as well as excitement in their work.

Not only were they new to Nichols Academy, in a larger sense, these preceptors were assembling a new and uniquely American educational system. There is every reason to believe they understood this. Based on the Nichols Academy's experience, educational historian Harriet Marr's conclusion that the "choice of a preceptor cannot be overestimated" is more than justified.[67] Usually preceptors were just out of college seeking personal direction and wanting to make some money while sacrificing a few comforts. They sought an introduction into teaching with an eye toward something more desirable. But their efforts deserve to be mentioned alongside those who pioneered textile mills and reaped the benefits of new technologies. They too, were builders of a new America contributing to an educational system that endured to the Civil War and influenced what was to occur long after that. While they exist only as names on a list, there can be little question that they contributed to the development of a favorable mind set toward education, tested many new ideas, and then took them from academy to academy. This was the nature and importance of their task.

One study of New England's academies finds 60 preceptors in these early years coming from Dartmouth, 35 from Yale, 21 from Amherst, and 16 from Harvard, as well as from other scattered institutions.[68] Of those who came to Nichols Academy, all appear to have been college graduates. The institutions of seven of the 25 pre-Civil War Nichols Academy preceptors can be easily identified. Three, Isaac Webb, Sanford Lawton, and Henry C. Morse, graduated from Yale, while four others – Alvin H. Washburn, James A. Clark,

Monroe Nichols, and John T. Clark – graduated from Williams College, Marietta College in Ohio, Wesleyan College, and Dartmouth College, respectively. In each case, they were carefully reviewed by a trustee committee. For instance, in the case in 1849 of Alvin H. Washburn, they found him "a gentleman of Liberal education and an experienced teacher having been two years a successful tutor in Marietta College where he graduated with distinguished honor" three years before. He was recommended by the Marietta president as a "gentleman and scholar, possessing every desirable qualification for a teacher of a classical and scientific school."[69] Washburn was hired in 1849, served as preceptor to 1851, and again in 1852. In many respects he was typical of the acceptable candidate.

Requirements and responsibilities of Nichols Academy's preceptors were established initially by the first Nichols Academy Board of Trustees. According to the *Constitution* of Nichols Academy:

> no person shall be chosen as an instructor in this [Nichols Academy] seminary, in the Christian Religion, of good natural abilities and literary requirements, of good acquaintance with human nature, of natural aptitude for instruction and government, and in the appointment of any instructor, regard shall be had to qualification only, without preference of kindred or friend, place of birth, education, or residence.
>
> It is required that the instructor's attention to the disposition of the minds and morals of the youth under his charge will exceed other cares as well considering, . . . It is therefore required that the instructor employ every effort to impress upon the minds of his pupils, their duty to God, their neighbors and themselves, and that he carefully delineate the odiousness of vice and the amicableness of virtue; while he exhibits piety and religion as the only sources of felicity in all the varying scenes of human life.[70]

Preceptors established the primary foundation stones for a morally proper educational environment. Nichols Academy, as an example, had morning Bible readings, required attendance at public worship, and generally offered non-sectarian Christianity as a middle road between sectarianism and secular public education.[71]

Between 1823 and 1860, a number of preceptors contributed to the Academy's success. Some can be easily identified. For instance, the first significant change in the nature of the Academy's academic program occurred in 1827–1828 under Preceptor H. Lowndes Street. That year the Academy formalized the women's program to be led by a preceptress, initiated the school's first formal announcements in newspapers in Worcester, Boston, Southbridge, and Brooklyn in Connecticut, and began discussion with the town of Dudley regarding a plan to provide secondary education to Dudley

Fig. 2.3. **Title Page,** *Catalogue . . . Nichols Academy . . . 1834* (Thompson, Conn.: George Roberts, Printer, 1834).

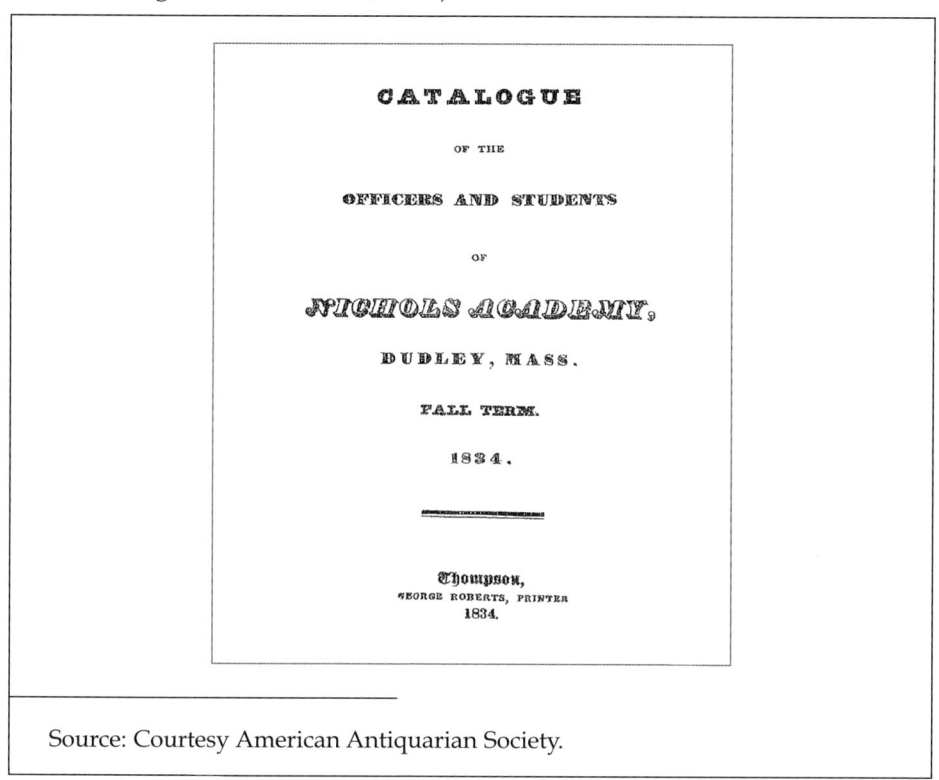

CATALOGUE

OF THE

OFFICERS AND STUDENTS

OF

NICHOLS ACADEMY,

DUDLEY, MASS.

FALL TERM.

1834.

Thompson,
GEORGE ROBERTS, PRINTER
1834.

Source: Courtesy American Antiquarian Society.

students twelve years of age and older.[72] In the process the Academy developed previously unstated admission requirements. Later in 1828, the Academy building was repainted. Clearly Street had been involved in decisions and discussions which contributed to significant institutional gains.

Benjamin I. Diefendorf, a Wesleyan graduate, served as preceptor from 1834 to 1836 and greatly strengthened the academic image of the Academy. Diefendorf reintroduced a public exhibition at the end of each term, published the first Academy catalogue, introduced several new assistants, and expanded the curriculum so that Academy scholars could participate in a program for common school teachers.[73] (See Fig. 2.3.) Through these and other efforts, he increased the enrollment from 74 to 114 "scholars." He also left other positive recollections as well. David Dwight, who attended during Diefendorf's years and later was an Academy trustee, remembered a delightful sleigh ride with the twenty-eight year old preceptor and other Academy students. Diefendorf's long history as a preceptor included stays at Wesleyan Academy in Wilbraham in Massachusetts, and other academies in Fort Plains, New York, and Mexico Academy in New York as well as serving as a minister in the Fort Plains area.

With enrollment totals fluctuating around one hundred students a year, academies such as Nichols, and Plainfield and Woodstock in Connecticut were vulnerable to the conditions of competition and obsolescence. For instance, when nearby Woodstock Academy in Connecticut experienced a number of problems, Woodstock students at Nichols increased from two to 18. However, when Woodstock Academy reopened in 1843, Nichols enrollment decreased from 127 to 89 and Woodstock was represented at Nichols by only three young scholars.[74] Plainfield, somewhat farther away, was about the same size as Nichols with an enrollment in 1851 of 119 and not surprisingly experienced similar challenges.[75]

Preceptors pushed Nichols to remain current and competitive despite financial hardships. In July 1844 when Samuel Bates became preceptor, he was offered "the whole" of the tuition payments, use of a suitable room for his private study, and could board at the Academy or elsewhere. Furthermore, the trustees agreed to his demands for a "Philosophical Apparatus" costing $120 and a pair of globes for $15 or $20 a piece. These were necessary to help him "clearly and forcibly illustrate the principles and those highly useful . . . for the benefit of the pupils and others."[76] He continued the expansion of the curriculum by offering lessons on the piano and in French.[77] His approach was to use the Academy catalogue as a means of promoting the Academy rather than merely presenting a record of its existence. For instance, his catalogues recognized Dudley for its pure air and its reputation as one of the healthiest towns in the Commonwealth and noted that "its retired situation renders it especially favorable to diligent study and good morals." And, for the first time, the catalogue referred directly to "those subjects, which are directly connected with the art of teaching . . . ."[78]

While Bates had helped the curriculum and educational offering with his technical improvements, there is no question that the trustees had legitimate concerns about their Academy building. This was their responsibility. They again found it in bad condition; "in a decaying state" as they put it.[79] Significant funds were necessary to make it serviceable. In 1851, the enrollment rose to 102, although it fell to 82 the following year.[80] The problem had become quite clear to the trustees by the end of the 1853 spring term when the enrollment numbers dropped to a low of 71.[81] They concluded that frequent changes in preceptors had hurt the institution and they simply would have to pay more to hire "a teacher of high qualifications" who would "do honor to the institution."[82] However, it was not until 1857 and three preceptors later that a solution appeared in the person of Monroe Nichols, a distant cousin of the Academy's founder, Amasa Nichols.[83]

More than any other preceptor to that point, Monroe Nichols understood the advantage of communicating directly to students at Nichols and to those interested in the Academy. His catalogues were informative and complete. In

Fig. 2.4. Nichols Academy Student Monthly Report, 1861

FORM OF MONTHLY REPORT.

NICHOLS ACADEMY.

Monthly Report of the Recitations, Attendance and Deportment of

For the year ending . . . . 18 . .

Absent frm. Ch.			Surveying,	
do. frm. Prayers,			Chemistry,	
do. from Class,			Rhetoric,	
No. times Tardy,			Bookkeeping,	
Deportment,*			Geometry,	
Spelling,			Algebra,	
Arithmetic,			Drawing,	
Geography,			Latin,	
Grammar,	.		Greek,	
History,			French,	
Physiology,			German,	
Nat. Philosophy,			Music,	
Intel. do.			Painting,	
Astronomy,			Composition,	
Geology,			Declamation,	

* Recitations and Deportment are marked from the number Five down to zero—Five denoting a high degree of excellence—zero, a total deficiency.

It is desirable that Parents and Guardians examine this Report with care; as it shows at a glance the Standing and Deportment of the Pupil.

M. NICHOLS, Principal.

Source: *Catalogue . . . Nichols Academy . . . Dudley, Mass., 1860–61*, NCA.

1858, he wrote that the course of instruction was "designed to embrace all that is necessary for common business, or for higher order of Collegiate or professional studies." Students who did well in the common branches were encouraged to "pursue Higher English or Classical studies."[84] As for the Academy's teaching program, he wrote that "many young men at this institution have teaching in view as their ultimate employment" and that classes were formed "for their special benefit and the various methods of teaching discussed . . . and illustrated."[85]

His later catalogues went further. When referring to the Academy's location, Monroe Nichols claimed that no similar institution existed "within many miles [and therefore] it supplies a necessary demand." Doing a bit of bragging, he added "as might be expected, [it] enjoys a high degree of prosperity." As for the character of the school and its scholars, he reemphasized the maturity of Nichols students by noting that "many [students] intend to become teachers, and the number pursuing classical studies is also large." He stressed the success of his "scholars" noting that in the last graduating class "nearly a dozen were going to College or Theological Seminaries."[86]

Consistent with his interest in better serving the student and his or her family, Principal Nichols also instituted a daily recording of "deportment, recitations and attendance" from which "the standing of each student is determined and is furnished to Parents and Guardians." (See Fig. 2.4.) This appears to have been the first time that students and parents were given information in this manner from the Academy. In his course of building the Academy's image, Monroe Nichols had at least four assistant teachers working with him teaching English and math, elocution and rhetoric, French and German, painting, and drawing and music.[87] He further added that his assistants at Nichols Academy were trying to learn the "real character" of their students to better assist them. (For a list of Nichols Academy Preceptors, see Appendix B.)

To suggest that Street, Diefendorf, Bates, and Monroe Nichols were the only successful Nichols preceptors simply is not correct. They all worked to improve the Academy program. They had help from members of the board of trustees who inventoried Academy possessions down to the last chair, assessed all the damages to the building and occasionally did all repairs, including building new "necessaries."[88] At the end of the first half of the nineteenth century, the Academy was continuing to keep two significantly different programs – the classical and the practical – together, or at least in the same school. This was one important legacy of Amasa Nichols, his fellow Universalists, and the later trustees who supported the nineteenth century academy.

CHAPTER 3

A Taste for Improvement

Time and changes in the educational environment led to a much matured academy at the end of its first forty years. For instance, Nichols Academy had come to accept a general Christian emphasis on individual conduct and moral piety. This thinking helped to redefine the Academy's position on individual morality, although it had little observable impact on the Universalist-designed curriculum. Furthermore, Nichols Academy's early success in remaining a contributing educational institution was a singular achievement.

Second, Nichols and many other rural academies provided young women with the opportunity for a secondary school education. Since Latin grammar schools before the academy had accepted only males, the education of significant numbers of young women was an important contribution to American society. Their experiences at rural Nichols Academy present a sharper picture of a somewhat provincial yet unique dimension of the Academy's educational development and the area's social history that is yet to be fully examined. The Nichols Academy history provides a better understanding of one aspect of the activities of young women in 19th century rural Massachusetts.

And, third, life and play was much in evidence at the Academy on Dudley Hill prior to 1860. So too was a picture of the Academy's role as a proud rural mentor and the subsequent emergence of Dudley Hill as an effective learning village. These components combined to establish a solid and unique base for the Dudley institution's next half century.

PIETY AND MORAL VIRTUE

Nichols Academy, as had been the case with almost all Massachusetts academies, was the product of a culture fully committed to Protestant Christianity. This culture touched all dimensions of human conduct and became the basis for moral and social progress.[1] Specific religious commitments had directed the development of earlier Latin grammar schools by creating an atmosphere of reverence, learning, guidance through prayer, in-class discussions of Sunday sermons, and condemnation of improper behavior. Usually the last day of each week at Latin grammar schools was spent catechizing or studying religious lessons.[2] This religious intensity was carried into the early nineteenth century where strong denominationalism continued to be the rule.

With time, however, the focus became less sectarian and began to shift from theology to individual morality. Nichols Academy's experience offers an excellent example of this change. The Universalist aim in 1819 had been to support an academy that intentionally avoided specific mention of religious tenets in its curriculum. However, it did promote the Bible and Universalist thinking through preaching and the encouragement of reason. It also included free schooling for future missionaries.

Initially Academy students had been expected to attend meetings in the Academy's Chapel led by Universalist preachers such as the Reverend Edward Turner, an Academy trustee. A Universalist meeting house eventually was constructed next door to the Academy in 1833.[3] And, within five years, the Academy was allowing its scholars to select from Congregationalist, Universalist, or Methodist services. The latter shared the Universalists' meeting house. Importantly, the Academy began to stress church attendance for the purpose of promoting individual moral conduct rather than for conversion or sectarian leadership. This adjustment was carefully explained in the 1861 Nichols Academy *Catalogue*:

> As this institution is supported by all Christian denominations, no sectarian principles of religion are inculcated. There are three religious societies in the place [Dudley Hill] – a Congregationalist, Methodist and Universalist. Each student is required to attend regularly the Church designated by parent or guardian. For those not connected with other Sabbath Schools there is a Bible Exercise on Sabbath morning in the Boarding House conducted by the principal.[4]

A willingness to accept the existence of three different religious societies points to attitudes quite different from those held by the Academy and those around it in 1819.[5] Also reflecting this change was the willingness of the Academy trustees to ask Congregational ministers, Reverends Abiel Williams and Joshua Bates, to serve as presidents of the Academy board of trustees during this same period.

When Nichols Academy was originally established in 1819, its mission was stated clearly: to promote piety and virtue and to instruct youth "in such language, and in such established arts and sciences, as directed by the Trustees."[6] Narrow denominationalism became less acceptable as society turned more to the business of commerce and began to reflect a greater diversity. Nonetheless, many still desired the moral lessons which resulted from close contact between education and religion.[7] From 1820 to 1860, the shift in educational focus was made from a theological foundation for religious education to a practical and secular moralism. The question for the Nichols Academy Board of Trustees was how to create an institution enjoying the presence of a moralizing impulse without relying on harsh dogma. This challenge usually was handed over to Academy preceptors.

Essentially, Nichols Academy relied for direction on day-to-day activities and traditional approaches to religion offered by the skills of proven teachers. The first advertisements for the Academy in 1828 refer to the practice of holding prayers before breakfast.[8] Nichols trustees looked to their preceptors to supervise the Academy students in developing moral character as well as providing academic preparation. For instance, the board applauded H. C. Morse, a preceptor in 1839–1840, as having an exemplary Christian character as well as achieving an "elevated rank" for his literary and scientific accomplishments.[9] Elisha W. Cook, preceptor in 1841, was seen providing "thorough and efficient instruction" thereby contributing to the moral and religious conduct and character of his students.[10] And, when the trustees hired Odgen Hall, they found him a teacher of "experience and success," who could help his students "form an elevated moral character."[11] Their goal was clear. It was the moral strength of the individual, not the specific nature of the sectarian commitment, that was critical. The spirit and morality embedded in a Protestant Christian culture were still present in most academies, including Nichols.[12]

State attitudes contributed significantly to the shifting of institutional climate as it pertained to the role of religion. Throughout the colonial period, the Commonwealth of Massachusetts had accepted the philosophy that it was the function of the state to promote both religion and education. The separation of state and church by the national and state constitutions then challenged old ways. In 1827, a Massachusetts act barred local school committees from approving textbooks that favored a specific sectarian position.[13] The Commonwealth then reemphasized its position with the disestablishment of religion in 1833. In short, although Massachusetts was eliminating the teaching of religious ideology in its public schools, a morally based culture remained an important factor in many private academies prior to the Civil War.

WOMEN AT THE OLD ACADEMY

Aside from broadening the Academy's approach from a rigid sectarian position to more moderate denominationalism, the Academy also contributed significantly to the education of young women. Local elementary schools had admitted young girls, but they could not go further since secondary education was not offered to females by Latin grammar schools. Beyond this level, there were few if any colleges available for women. Nonetheless, academies such as Nichols did accept young women. This was not a radical change since Universalists generally supported gender equality. However, it was an important step in America's educational history and a significant step for women in their efforts to gain equality.

In the case of Nichols Academy, two young girls had been among the first group of seven students formally enrolled in Amasa Nichols' school in May 1819. That summer and before the first fall term began, a total of six young girls and thirteen boys had enrolled. This was an occasion of note both for women and for the Academy. In rural Massachusetts prior to the American Revolution, the only schooling for a young girl, apart from home schooling, had been the district elementary school. These small rural district schools with wooden benches and two relatively brief two- to three-month terms each year generally were available for students from five to fifteen years of age. This elementary school experience covered what usually is referred to as the three "R's."

Males did have choices after finishing elementary schools. Those living near a population center or willing to travel to large communities such as Boston or Springfield could attend a Latin grammar school if interested in a program leading to a college or university for a professional or religious life. Women did not have this choice. When an entirely new secondary school – the academy – appeared in rural Massachusetts, New England, and elsewhere after the American Revolution, doors opened to girls as well as boys. This greatly expanded the educational universe for American society. Certainly this was the case for the communities around Nichols Academy.

Historians of education have a number of well-reasoned explanations for women's interest in attending the young academies. They cite increased leisure time, a need for education as a preparation for motherhood, a commitment to assist one's husband and to protect the home.[14] Some have argued that the main purpose of a woman's education was to be a better housekeeper, companion and mother as well as to become a more involved citizen.[15] However, many young women just wanted the opportunity to learn.

An examination of female students at "old" Nichols Academy points to two phases of women's education. The first features their actual involvement in the Academy itself. This relates to their number, skills, and ability to participate and contribute to the life of the Academy. The second deals with the wider questions of how a woman's experience at the small academy both affected and reflected attitudes regarding gender differences. Intellectual competition with males was one thing, acceptance by a male-dominated society was quite another. A careful assessment of the role played by rural academies such as Nichols in educating women contributes to the ongoing process of evaluating the status of women during this period. Much that has been available for historians has been based on experiences at all-girl seminaries such as Troy Female Seminary in New York, Hartford Female Seminary, and Mount Holyoke in Massachusetts.[16] The Nichols experience as a rural, coeducational academy provides a different context.

There had been little, if any, formal discussion by the Nichols Academy Board of Trustees regarding the admission of women in 1819. The missionary approach of the Universalists required the inclusion of everyone. Women, as well as men, had to be directly involved in the Universalist cause, if it was to succeed. Over the eight years between 1819 and 1827, approximately 23 percent of the total student body was made up of young women.[17] This percentage increased with time. When the town of Dudley agreed to send its students to the Academy in 1828, both the total number of students and the number of female students jumped significantly.[18] Available enrollment statistics from the years 1828 to 1856 show that approximately 40 percent of documentable academy students were young women (506 females out of an identifiable student body of 1,260, see Appendix C).[19] In fact, the Academy probably could not have survived without their participation – and their tuition.

Many young women, a large portion of whom came from Dudley, immediately flocked to the Academy when they got the chance. By 1860, female enrollment numbers in a single term occasionally exceeded male enrollment. This eventually changed, but the numbers themselves reflect an obvious enthusiasm that cannot be dismissed.[20] To facilitate this interest, the Academy briefly established formal ties with the town of Dudley, advertized the opening of a department of "Female Education," and hired a preceptress formerly at Groton Academy.[21] Whatever differences that existed in the treatment of males and females at Nichols Academy were based primarily on traditional thinking about gender limitations and not on the performance of the students involved. For instance, the assumption that women could not perform well in mathematics caused the Academy trustees along with Dudley town officials to exempt them from Academy entrance requirements that required a knowledge of five parts of arithmetic: addition, subtraction, multiplication, division, and reduction.[22]

The belief that women could not meet the Academy mathematics requirement is challenged by at least one documented case in 1830. That year Dolly Corbin of Dudley completed a workbook that demonstrated her ability to master a number of rules, complete formal answers, and finish all exercises through the Golden Rule of Three. Corbin's still-existing workbook is a splendid example of work that meets the highest standards.[23] Undoubtedly there were other similar cases. These instances call into question the long-held view that mathematics was "unthinkable for the poor delicate female mind."[24]

That young women were interested in education beyond elementary school was verified by the large numbers who attended Nichols Academy. This too may have been somewhat of a surprise. Aside from enrollment numbers, there is much anecdotal material that establishes the existence of significant levels of ability and interest in learning on the part of young women. For instance, most believed that women were not going to take any subjects offered in the Academy's Classical course since there were few colleges for them to attend. Despite this, even in the first few years of the Academy, women did take the Classical course. Two years after Nichols Academy opened its doors, Mary Campbell of Dudley registered for the Classical course; three years later, Jane Foster followed.[25] Still more evidence that challenges the theory of intellectual inadequacy is contained in the 1835 Academy *Catalogue*. Lucy Ann Harris of Oxford was listed as one of nine Latin scholars. Jane Fay Bemis of Dudley was one of three Greek scholars that year.[26] There is no record that they went on to college or ever intended to do so. Rather, they sought the experience of learning, something not possible without the Academy.

While young women at Nichols Academy were making progress in expanding their intellectual opportunities, attitudes promoting a secondary status for women remained in place. It was difficult to change a males-only focus. Nichols Academy catalogues frequently referred to opportunities for its "young men," despite the fact that nearly half of the student body was composed of young women.[27] The 1857–1858 Academy *Catalogue* indicated that lectures on the art of teaching were available for "many young men" interested in teaching. This statement apparently overlooked a large number of Nichols Academy women preparing to teach in district elementary schools. On a few occasions, a reference to "both genders" was made.[28] Nonetheless, the only direct or complete references to women in attendance at the Academy are found in the lists of enrolled students contained in Academy catalogues.

Successes experienced by women in academies have led one historian to note that "higher education of women in the United States clearly dates from the establishment of academies . . . ."[29] While this conclusion certainly is correct, this progress did not successfully challenge the concept of separate spheres, whereby women were envisioned as existing on different and perhaps lesser levels than men. The continual expansion of women's education, however, was increasing opportunities for women in this new society. Young women no longer were locked into farm work; they could teach in elementary schools for a salary. Many did. The same can be said of the young farm girls from northern New England, who left to work in the textile mills of Lowell, Massachusetts, then took their savings and went west to teach. Nonetheless, while the potential to move and become independent increased for women, it remained difficult to advance beyond boundaries still being set by traditional male thinking.

This progress in women's education, as was the case with other Academy experiences, achieved substantial lasting results. Public high schools of the post-1850s era did not have to deal with potentially thorny questions regarding the ability of women to meet academic requirements on a secondary school level. These questions had been answered at the Academy. The Nichols Academy experience gave Dudley area women a better sense of potential and direction. When the "Age of the Academy" began to wane by the 1860s, young women were being accepted in free public high schools as a result of impressive efforts over the previous fifty years. Their battle did not end, but tangible gains had been registered.

LIFE, PLAY AND EXPENSES

There are no fully developed commentaries regarding the adventures of Academy scholars on Dudley Hill. The Reverend Charles L. Goodell, however, provides a number of brief glimpses into Academy life over a fifty year period. Goodell, who lived on Dudley Hill, wrote in his *Black Tavern Tales* that he liked to see the arrival of the older boys in the winter terms because it meant "there was likely something to be doing," although he was not specific.[30] Mostly Academy scholars spent their time on the farm when not at the Academy. However, there were others such as Charles Goodell's brothers, Anson and Edwin, who learned shoemaking as a trade. As a result, their education combined practical and academic learning experiences in a way that would have pleased early academy promoters such as Benjamin Franklin.

Some of the most insightful and sensitive observations regarding the early Academy experience are provided by the letters of Anson Goodell, Reverend Goodell's brother. An enlistee in the Union Army in the Civil War, Anson wrote home reflecting on his life at home and at Nichols Academy. He mentioned his little studio where he encountered "a difficult problem in Arithmetic, Algebra, or Geometry [that] had cost hours of painful toil . . . knotty passages of Virgil . . . [that kept him up] long after the 9 o'clock bell hour has struck the hour for retiring or midnight's dull hours."[31]

Anson Goodell's education and experiences at the Academy also were reflected in his letters about the Civil War. In one splendid sentence, he summed up his feelings: "To our generation is committed the important trust of stabilizing the Government on a broader stronger more enduring basis of universal liberty, unconditional freedom to all, black and white, and we ought to see well that we discharge our trust in a manner worthy of the all-important task committed to our hands."[32] His ability to articulate his thoughts about his role in society correctly suggests the educational contributions of the old Academy as well as the measure and maturity of the person.

Although official Academy records do not mention the details of life and play at the Academy, evidence suggests that its scholars were little different than those who attended similar schools long after the Academy's heyday. There is no question that Academy boys and girls had fun; undoubtedly some of it caused occasional discomfort for Dudley Hill citizens.

Again, the recollections of Reverend Goodell are revealing. For instance, he commented that the bell Anson Goodell fondly remembered frequently was a target for rambunctious Academy lads. One favorite stunt, probably pulled at least once a year, involved turning the academy bell upside-down during the coldest winter night and filling it with water, thereby encasing the clapper in ice. When the bell ringer pulled the rope, there was no sound – and the ice-filled bell did not ring that day. Boiling water eventually freed the clapper from its ice-bound position, but the next few days saw many smiles on an otherwise cold student body.[33] Spur-of-the-moment pranks were always part of the picture. Reverend Goodell recounted occasions when students managed to raise items such as sleds or other articles to the Academy's ridge pole. Penalties were not part of his story, although some punishments may have been involved.

Neither Academy records nor recollections refer directly to punishments for disciplinary reasons although Principal Monroe Nichols had a category for deportment on his Monthly Report Forms after 1860.[34] There are no specific statements regarding imposed penalties or punishments. Without documentation discussing the issue, it is difficult to draw any conclusions. There is no question, however, that occasional incidents requiring substantial punishment did occur in New England academies.

In her book, *Old New England Academies*, Harriet Webster Marr provides actual instances of the presence of corporal punishment including flogging, the use of raw hide, and solitary confinement.[35] According to Marr, most academies limited the use of corporal punishment. Some preceptors such as Timothy Dwight at Greenfield Hill in Connecticut felt it was ineffective for almost everyone. Some instituted a demerit system. Most preceptors, according to Marr, believed that the primary purpose of a proper reaction should be admonishment, not punishment. This was the better way to promote moral and intellectual development. It is Marr's conclusion that academy students probably were studious and ambitious and less inclined to warrant punishment.[36]

As for organized sports, the Reverend Goodell describes a game they played at Nichols Academy called "round ball" that descended from the

English game of "rounders," something like baseball today.[37] It was played with a moderately pitched soft ball and, from Reverend Goodell's description, required throwing the ball at the base runner ("soaking" or striking him) to get him out. "Round ball" was also known as the "Massachusetts Game" or "town ball" at the height of its popularity in the late 1850s. This sport was played on a sixty-foot square field without any designated foul territory. The batter or striker stood midway between first and fourth base, with ten to fourteen players on a side, and the ball was in play wherever it was hit – either in front of or behind the batter. There was no "foul" territory. The "Massachusetts Game" was replaced with what baseball historian John Thorn suggests was a more proper, less aggressive, more gentlemanly game called the "New York Game."[38] The New York version eventually did away with the Massachusetts game.

Reverend Goodell recalled that the Academy had a "great" team called the "Nipmucks" after the local Native Americans. At this time they were seeking greater recognition from state and federal authorities. Undoubtedly Nipmuc supporters were found in the Dudley Hill area, once a part of Nipmuc lands.

During this time period, members of competing New England teams had begun to select colors to identify their school teams. For instance, in the late 1850s the Harvard University crew members put on crimson scarves to identify themselves when in competition. Some athletes from Williams College in Williamstown, Massachusetts, wore purple ribbons selected to give them identity. Both institutions, as well as others including Nichols Academy, eventually formalized their colors although many were changed over the course of the 19th century.

As for Nichols Academy, official trustee meeting records of the Academy do not exist for the period 1874 to 1906 making it difficult to verify the colors of the Academy, if they existed. In fact, however, ribbons identified as black and orange were found on an Academy diploma awarded in 1878. Similarly colored basketball uniforms were introduced in 1904.[39] This evidence and similarity alone suggest a relationship between what appeared to be Academy colors at the beginning of the 20th century and the first Nichols colors perhaps appearing in the early 1860s.

The team played on a field next to the Village Common between the town meeting house and the Academy building, undoubtedly cheered on by classmates. Until its series was interrupted by war, the team competed with a neighboring team known as the Uptons, although, like so many things in memory, the precise details are somewhat vague.[40] Many contests took so long to score the one hundred runs required to win, that games frequently had to be called before they were finished. Perhaps it was not the score of the game that was important, rather it simply was the fun of it. This changed abruptly when "the boys of '61" began drilling on the Common under Principal Monroe

Nichols.[41] The shouts from the ballfield were replaced, as Reverend Goodell tells it, by "the hoarse yell of the battlefield" that came from places such as Bull Run and Gettysburg. An era had moved on.[42]

Certainly there were other events that occupied time and gave much pleasure. One former student, David Dwight, recalled a "jolly good time" on a sleigh ride with his classmates and Preceptor Diefendorf, an incident probably repeated hundreds of times.[43] Reverend Goodell's account also did not ignore the social side of Academy life. His brief but meaningful reference to a "Sociable" that occurred once a term suggests an eagerly anticipated event. Although there was no dancing, these were special occasions. His recollections of these "Sociables" were still very clear years later although he provided few actual details. According to his account, "Nature did [then] for the girls what art is invoked to do to their grandchildren and did it better!" Writing in his twilight years, his prose did not shield his feelings. As he went on: "By standards erected in wiser and less happy days, those were unconventional and bucolic sports [that they played], but Miss One-and-Twenty, will your recollections make your heart thrill as ours do when you are Mistress One-and-Sixty?"[44]

In one sense, the Goodell children differed from the others on the Hill. Anson Goodell's living accommodations as well as those of his two brothers, Edwin and Charles, were not the usual fare for Academy students. Their home in the Black Tavern, built in 1804 and still standing, was a long-time family residence of the Healy's and then the Goodell's. Arguably, it was the most imposing house at the top of Dudley Hill. If "scholars" did not live at home as the Goodells did, they might board in the Academy building itself, or, after 1873, in the new Academy boarding house. Others simply made boarding arrangements with home owners around the Hill. The Reverend Goodell believed that fewer than half the Nichols students were able to afford boarding in the Academy. Initially, the boarding week was seven days, eventually a five-day week also became available.[45]

By the mid-1830s, perhaps as many as 30 scholars could board in the Academy, a practice that began in 1823 with a smaller number. Those who could pay the boarding costs found ten rooms available in the Academy building, along with a separate room for eating and a kitchen under the steward's control. For instance, in 1834 there were 15 "scholars" boarding with Mrs. Day, the Academy steward.[46] The Academy's boarding operation was run by the steward whose responsibilities included preparing meals for which he or she received a monthly food "allowance" from the trustees. (What was not spent on food from this allowance could be kept by the steward.) Both the preceptor and the steward were supplied with quarters, frequently at no cost, in a building that must have been crowded at times.

In his *Black Tavern Tales*, Reverend Goodell recalled that all available rooms in the village were occupied by farm boys and girls arriving Monday mornings and leaving Friday nights. Many walked five to ten miles to get to Dudley Hill. Some came by stage coach. After 1836 they could come by rail to nearby Webster and then take a carriage or walk the three miles to the Academy. Although they might eat with the family where they boarded, many students brought their own food and linen from home. Their supplies included a stock of bread, beans, doughnuts and pies. In Reverend Goodell's opinion, "many a stomach was permanently ruined by the boys and girls who boarded themselves." He did concede, however, that their fare on Dudley Hill probably resulted in less gastronomical grief than what might have been caused later on by "a chef and a high-ball mixer" in a more advanced society.[47]

Surprisingly, despite the problems caused by the aging Academy building, enrollment was expanding as the Civil War commenced. The total number of enrollees during the 1861–1862 year reached 267 (153 males and 114 females) from 35 towns in four states. This was to be the highest enrollment in the Academy's history. Ten years before, 102 students (47 males and 55 females) were enrolled from 16 communities in three states.[48] When compared with enrollments at nearby academies, Nichols' totals were about the same as Plainfield Academy, but fewer than the 296 students enrolled at Leicester Academy in 1848.[49] While a comparison of academies is hard to make, it is probable that the typical Massachusetts academy had 40 to 45 students enrolled each term with two teachers. Nichols appears to fall into this category.[50]

A number of important individuals passed through the old Academy. Several children of industrialist Samuel Slater attended the Academy as did the offspring of one of Slater's partners, Edward Howard.[51] Less well known at the time, Hezekiah Conant, who was from the northern part of Dudley, attended Nichols Academy for several terms over a number of years between 1841 and 1851.[52] Thirty years later, he was to rebuild the Academy. And there were others, including the Reverend Zephaniah Baker, a writer, historian, builder, and later Nichols Academy trustee. As Reverend Goodell put it, "there were many who climbed to the high places of opportunity and power through development which the academy had provided. . . . there were half a hundred men who had a college education because of the influence of Nichols Academy. . . ."[53] Scholars from the Academy are reported to have selected a number of different colleges including Williams, Yale, and Wesleyan over the half century ending in 1860.

Few academies could have survived without income from tuition. Nichols was no exception. In rural America, academies provided education to scattered Americans who were willing to pay for what was not available otherwise. For a young man or woman entering the Classical course at Nichols Academy in

Fig. 3.1. Nichols Academy Tuition-Boarding Costs, 1819–1861

	1819	1835	1850	1861
TUITION (by term)				
Classical Course	$4.00	$4.33	$6.00	$6.75
English Course	$3.00	$3.33	$4.67	$4.50
Other				
Drawing/Painting		$4.33	$2.00	$2.00
Philosophy		$3.33		
Chemistry		$3.33		
Math		$3.33		
Higher English			$5.33	$6.00
Piano			$10.00	$10.00
French & Italian			$2.00	$2.00
Inc. Exp				$0.20
BOARDING (expenses in Academy building only)				
7-day week	$1.33-$1.50*	$1.50	$1.50	$2.25
5-day week	Not Available		$1.33	$1.50

includes washing

Sources: *Constitution of Nichols Academy; Catalogue . . . Nichols Academy . . . 1835,* NCA; Ibid., 1849–50; Ibid., 1860–61.

1819, the cost for one term including tuition, room, and board was $20.50; the three-term charge was $61.50. These same arrangements, tuition, room, and board, nearly forty years later cost $30.00 for one term and $90.00 for the year. Similarly, charges for the common English course were $19.50 for tuition, room and board for one term and $58.50 for three terms in 1819 and $28.67 and $86.00 in 1856. If a five-day boarding week was selected, costs were slightly reduced. In comparison, fees at Plainfield Academy in Connecticut were somewhat higher than those at Nichols.[54] In 1832, Plainfield charged $7.00 for its Classical course and $4.00 for the English course compared with Nichols charges of $4.33 and $3.33, respectively. Weekly boarding fees at Plainfield were $1.50 to $1.75 as opposed to somewhat lower fees of $1.33 to $1.50 for the Dudley academy. (See Fig. 3.1.)

These charges probably will not stagger the modern reader. Nonetheless, the average annual income of a non-farming American family in 1860 was about $360.[55] Disposable income for a farm family was considerably less. Most laborers could earn $1.00 a day, if they had work. Furthermore, many families faced the prospects of having two and three children, perhaps more, eligible for the Academy in the same year. Sometimes this problem was solved by sending a different family member each term thus distributing the costs as well as the educational benefits. Nonetheless, the cost of a full year's education might be equal to 25 percent of an average family income. Some simply could not afford the expense. It might also be argued that those who attended the Academy were more responsible than the average population because of the costs involved, but this is difficult to prove.

THE LEARNING VILLAGE

A year or so after the Academy's first classes in 1819, Amasa Nichols wrote to Nichols Academy trustee, Reverend Edward Turner, that "anything you can do toward furnishing Scholars is important."[56] This need for more students never changed. The trustees placed the institution's first regional notice in newspapers in Worcester, Boston, and Brooklyn in Connecticut, in 1828.[57] (See Fig. 2.1.) The first Nichols Academy catalogues appeared in 1834. (See Fig. 2.3.) These small ten-to-twelve page publications listed the names of the scholars, members of the board of trustees, and instructors (preceptors and assistants). They also provided tuition and board costs, terms of enrollment, rules, and textbooks used in subjects.[58] And, since grade reports were not formally given or even recorded, these publications provided the student with actual proof of attendance.

Not surprisingly, Academy catalogues took on a more promotional style and role in the mid-1840s when they began to spell out the institution's strong points. For instance, the 1845 *Nichols Academy Catalogue* featured the Academy's location, geographical advantages and the positive impact it had on the educational experience. It is noted that Nichols Academy was nearly three miles from the Webster depot of the Norwich and Worcester Railroad. This catalogue also pointed out that the school's elevation and "pure air" made it one of the "most healthy towns in the Commonwealth" and that its "retired" location offered an environment conducive to "diligent study habits and good morals."[59] Five years later, Nichols Academy was said to be an excellent place for scholars "to devote their entire attention to studies preparatory to entering College."[60]

Over these early years, the town of Dudley changed significantly. Once centered primarily in the village of Dudley Hill around the Academy, clusters of houses now appeared along the French River in emerging mill villages such as Perryville, Chaseville, Merino Village, Tufts Village to the north and West Dudley to the west. All were two to three miles from Dudley Hill. These textile villages were replacing Dudley Hill as the town's economic and social centers. In turn, the Dudley Hill village re-emerged as a specialized community: a learning village. By 1850, the Academy and the village of Dudley Hill had grown together for the dual purpose of education and survival. All involved agreed on the importance of education. The Academy made its programs available to everyone and few in this village did not spend at least one term there. Students who completed an Academy course frequently taught in district elementary schools contributing to stronger ties. Preceptors chosen by the trustees ran the academic program usually for a two-year period. In the process they introduced new ideas from colleges such as Yale, Williams, Marietta, Wesleyan and Dartmouth. Their thinking automatically spread throughout the village's boarding network and into the Dudley community.

Dudley Hill developed as a learning village because its citizens and the Academy students shared many essential values.[61] Most students came from rural environments. In the pre-Civil War period, most were Protestants. Scholars attended services at one of three churches or societies – Universalist, Congregational, or Methodist – all then on Dudley Hill. The fact that a number of Academy trustees, from Amasa Nichols and John Brown to the Reverend Dr. Charles L. Goodell, lived on the Hill also helped to secure the relationship between the Academy and its village. Moreover, the Academy had become the educational flagship for the entire region resulting in a legitimate sense of community pride on the part of the villagers.

Dudley center had become a necessary and vital part of the Academy's existence by providing boarding accommodations for students. This led to extra income for Dudley Hill home owners and provided reasonable accommodations for the students. As a result, the activities at the Academy automatically became part of the daily routine and gossip of the village and this continued well beyond the 1890s. Heads of Dudley Hill households and their families logically became an integral and important part of the Nichols Academy family. Virtually every Dudley family had sacrificed to have one or more of its members attend the Academy. Nearly every Hill family had boarded one or more Academy students.

Much anecdotal evidence suggests that Nichols Academy was an effective and respected institution. Its survival and general community support testify to this. For one, the Trustees and preceptors of the Academy believed in their institution. In 1860, in an admittedly promotional effort, the Academy catalogue noted the high demand for its services and believed it was a highly successful educational institution.[62] Others spoke approvingly of the Academy. The Reverend Joshua Bates of the Dudley Congregational Church and a former president of Middlebury College, wrote in 1853: ". . . this school, on account of its favorable location, is unquestionably destined to exert a still higher and more extended influence on the inhabitants of this town and the surrounding community." Reverend Bates believed that the denominations on Dudley Hill had to work together since the three churches existed "where one would have been sufficient to accommodate all. . . ."[63] He also served as president of the Nichols Academy Board of Trustees.

While the free, public high school appeared to some ready to challenge the very essence of the Academy, others disagreed.[64] The two educational themes around which Nichols Academy had been formed – life-directed learning and preparation for college and theological schools – remained central to its approach to education. These themes were tied together to form a remarkably strong and enduring learning community. The firmness with which Amasa Nichols had planted his institution on Dudley Hill was now crucial to its continued existence.

But the Nichols Academy of the 1850s was far different from the school of Amasa Nichols and the New England Universalists that existed between 1819 and 1823. The first Academy's purpose had been to promote Universalism by educating the children of Universalists throughout New England with a curriculum written by New England's most prominent Universalist preachers. Theirs had been an impressive although tenuous beginning in occasionally unfriendly and challenging surroundings. Perhaps they had been too ambitious. Although progress was frequently reported to the New England Universalist convention, inadequate finances, disagreements within Universalist ranks, and poor communication between Universalist leaders in the Boston area and the Academy in Dudley weakened these early ties. Then too, the financially besieged Amasa Nichols was a burden after 1822. In short, the arrangement between the New England Universalists and the local trustees proved to be unworkable; the effort of the Universalists to operate the Academy did not succeed. Nonetheless, the Academy did not close its doors.

Essentially, the post-1823 Academy remained private and independent and continued to be governed by a board of trustees. This governing group was now composed of Congregationalists, Methodists, and Universalists resulting in necessary cooperation rather than conflict. Most lived in the Dudley Hill area. Nichols "scholars" were still required to attend church on Sunday but could now select from one of three religious societies on Dudley Hill. The "old" Academy, unlike the Universalist Academy, had no specific interest in developing preachers. Rather, the goal was to encourage the development of morally strong individuals. Importantly, the curriculum developed in 1819 was kept in place and continued to focus on a dual program – the Classical and common English courses – with additional sciences, languages, and higher levels of English joining core subjects.

Change also was evident in the relationship between the Academy and public education. Initially, the Universalist Academy had received little broad local support although it had been given some state assistance. This changed in 1827 when the Academy, led by local Academy trustees, agreed to enroll Dudley students with the tax-payer responsible for taking care of the negotiated tuition. While this agreement with the town continued only for one year, a similar arrangement was to be made in 1871. Clearly the Academy's relations with the town of Dudley improved during the "old" Academy period.

This was not the case with Nichols Academy's relations with the state. In its first years, the Academy had received a state grant consisting of land which was available to support Massachusetts academies. The partnership relationship gradually changed. Overtime, Nichols Academy's requests to the state for funding went unanswered. The Academy was no longer part of a quasi-public system that had given the Academy state land in 1825. Nonetheless, many understood what the academies had accomplished.

Without doubt, the "old" Academy had a significant impact on everyone with whom it had contact. It helped those within its reach to loosen the bands of sectarianism which had existed since the school began. It made the individual a focal point through close personal contact. This established a model to be followed. Then too, the old school gave young women, as well as young men, the opportunity to learn – and for improvement. Young women could show their potential although time was necessary for long-existing cultural realities to adjust. That this eventually could occur was due in part to the earlier contributions of the Academy. Schools such as Nichols had "created a taste for improvement," as a speaker at Gilmanton Academy in New Hampshire in 1859 stated in an effective summation of the contributions made by academies.[65] Improvement came in many ways. Certainly it was crucial for the future of American secondary school education as well as stimulating both elementary and higher education. In the process it worked to change American society.

CHAPTER 4

A New Academy Emerges

Between 1860 and 1900, the United States was recovering from the sectional strife that had led to the Civil War and Reconstruction while well on the way to becoming a world industrial power. Both accelerated industrial growth and the economic ascendency of the North. All aspects of the American society – agriculture, commerce, manufacturing, transportation and communication – expanded dramatically. Immigration added to America's population and increased the size of its urban areas while bringing the newcomers necessary to promote and support this growth. They joined the hard-working Americans who had built antebellum America. Together, they forced demographic change into all corners of the still young nation. At the same time, many war-weary Americans looked away from the challenges of the previous half-century, such as the anti-slavery crusade and civil war, toward less idealistic but more lucrative goals made possible by America's mushrooming industrial society and exploding wealth.

Not surprisingly, these developments greatly affected secondary education in the United States. In the early 1860s Nichols Academy was enrolling more students than ever before – or after. At the same time, the Academy was beginning to experience significant problems. The Academy building constructed in 1818 and 1819 needed extensive repairs. Beyond this, the clamor of public school supporters for free education together with the desire of the Massachusetts Board of Education to control secondary education in the Commonwealth combined to threaten the existence of private academies. This led to vigorous and revealing debates between the supporters of the two radically different approaches to nineteenth century secondary education in Massachusetts: the public way and the academy way.

Two vital developments greatly influenced the course and character of the Nichols Academy that emerged after the 1860s. The first was an agreement with the town of Dudley in 1871 making Nichols Academy the high school of Dudley. The second was the complete rebuilding of the Nichols Academy campus by Hezekiah Conant, a former Academy student and Dudley resident, now a successful Rhode Island industrialist, who joined the Nichols Academy Board of Trustees in 1874. In the short run, the town of Dudley, along with Hezekiah Conant, provided the structure, direction, and financial support necessary to send the Academy forward into the first decade of the next century. In the long run, however, Nichols Academy was committed to offering a high school program dictated by the Massachusetts Board of Education as well as a preparatory school program that had to conform to the admissions requirements of a growing number of colleges and universities. In the past, Nichols Academy had developed its own programs and goals based on a perception of the needs of its society; this was going to change. It could not remain a "mixed" corporation for long.[1] The old academy was about to disappear.

TRANSITION DECADE

Those concerned about the Academy's future had reason to be apprehensive as it entered the mid-1860s. The Academy building was in poor condition and enrollments were beginning to decline with the growth of area public high schools. If this was not troubling enough, the Massachusetts Board of Education was working against private academies seeing them standing in the way of secondary school development in Massachusetts.

A period of declining enrollments at Nichols Academy had begun as early as 1850 when total registrations dropped below 100 students a year. Furthermore, the number of students attending for more than one term during the course of a year continued to remain small. In the 1850–1851 school year, 76 percent of the total student enrollment that year attended only one term (out of three). The following year the percentage attending just one term actually increased to 83 percent. The 1851–1852 winter term saw only ten students enrolled; all were males. This phenomena, as strange as it now seems, reflected earlier elementary school attendance patterns, the emergence of public secondary schools, and the continuing tendency of some "scholars" to "flit" or move from one academy to another each term.

Going from one academy to another, or "flitting," was an interesting and fairly common phenomenon. The experience of Albert Paine of East Woodstock, Connecticut, provides a good example. Paine began his schooling at Monson Academy in Monson, Massachusetts, in 1834 when he was fifteen years old. Monson had been incorporated in 1804. After Monson, he appeared at Nichols Academy. Then Paine went back to Monson and, finally, he went to Plainfield Academy in Connecticut. He eventually headed for Yale College and graduated in 1841. All this was accomplished in eight years.[2] And this experience was not as unique as it seems.[3]

During the years just prior to the Civil War, Nichols Academy's geographical range of students had slowly become smaller. The problems of a falling enrollment also had to be faced. In 1850–1851, 16 towns had been represented in the Academy enrollment. The next year there were only 11. More specifically, the Academy's primary enrollment now was coming from six or seven towns within a ten-mile radius of Dudley. Roughly 76 percent of the first year students in 1850–1851 and 94 percent of the next year's students came from Dudley, Oxford, Webster, Charlton, Southbridge, and Thompson and the Woodstocks in Connecticut.[4] Between 1850 and 1853, scholars from Dudley made up more than 50 percent of the student body – with more females than males enrolled.[5]

Principal Monroe Nichols and his assistants brought the Academy back from the brink of collapse after 1857, although the Civil War eventually ended his contributions to the Academy and shortened his life. The "old" Academy recovered dramatically by 1862 under Principal Nichols' leadership with much of the old school remaining. When academies had extended periods of success, it generally was due to popular preceptors who remained over long spans of time. For instance, Exeter Academy had five preceptors in 77 years; Andover had only six in 82 years.[6] Monroe Nichols proved the value of this extended leadership at Nichols Academy.

At the end of the Civil War, control of the Academy was still in the hands of a board of trustees with deep Dudley roots. The curriculum continued, as the *Catalogue* in 1858 had put it, "to embrace all that is necessary as a preparation for common business, or for higher order of Collegiate, or professional studies."[7] The Academy also supported the continuing interest of its scholars in teaching.[8] And, for all its adjustments, the Academy was still "in one building – a large and commodious structure – in which the principal acting also as steward, resides with the boarding pupils."[9] This was not for long.

Monroe Nichols was introducing a number of adjustments that pointed the school away from 1819 and toward the "new" Academy. For one, Nichols and his assistants started to work with students to design individual approaches to their education. New thinking called for the principal and his assistants to put themselves in the parents' place and to require students to "observe habits of order, neatness, punctuality and diligence . . . to regulate their whole conduct by the acknowledged principles of true politeness."[10] Monroe Nichols urged parents and guardians to register their children at the beginning of each term and to be sure they stayed until the term's end so the Academy could have a maximum instructional impact. Apparently it had been possible to walk in and out of an academic term at any time.[11] Further, the Academy announced a tougher standard for conduct noting that "no student will be retained whose influence is found to be pernicious" although this term was not discussed further.[12]

Under Monroe Nichols, the Academy was more aggressive in developing its academic program. In his opinion, basic subjects, such as reading, spelling, and penmanship provided the necessary foundation for a substantial education and he said so. Principal Nichols believed a student could pursue Higher English or Classical studies only after achieving success in basic areas. While the common English and Classical courses were the main courses, other formal program designations now included Higher Mathematics, Natural Science, Belles Lettres and Moral Science. Monthly reports featuring grades from zero to five for recitations, attendance and deportment were sent to parents and guardians to assist in evaluating student progress.[13] (See Fig. 2.4.)

In the five years between 1857 and 1862 under Principal Nichols, the Academy implemented a graded system of instruction, granted certificates, made examinations public, formally graduated students who reached the end of their programs, organized lyceums, and encouraged a debating society.[14] Reverend Charles Goodell wrote that "nothing paid higher dividends than the Old Lyceum." He felt that these sessions developed the critical skills required to preside over conventions, conferences and legislatures.[15] In the past, students had left the Academy either when accepted by a college or university based on a qualifying examination or when they or their families decided that one's formal education was over. This too was changing as the Academy began to recognize students who completed programs.

Not surprisingly, the Academy's aggressive institutional development resulted in record enrollment numbers. Between 1860 and 1863, from 244 to 267 students enrolled for at least one term each year.[16] Despite this success, a careful analysis of available records reveals subtle and unfavorable underlying changes. For one, the percentage of women enrolled began to decrease noticeably falling from nearly 50 percent to 40 percent from 1861 to 1863. Secondly, the number of towns represented in the student body started to decline. Communities within ten miles of the Academy, including Dudley, now provided 73 percent of the total enrollment for each year. In short, the geographic footprint of the Academy continued to shrink despite increased totals. (See Appendix D for selected town representation at the Academy.)

The American Civil War disrupted the lives of all Americans. Those involved in the Academy – former students, the student body, the preceptors, and members of the learning community – suffered, as did most Americans, from the tragic consequences of war previously unknown to most of their generation. Although all former Nichols students involved in the Civil War have not been identified, several cases speak for missing friends and colleagues. One former Nichols Academy student was Sullivan Ballou, made famous by PBS and Ken Burns in their production, *The Civil War*. Ballou's unforgettable "Letter to Sarah" provided this documentary with vital themes of love and duty. Ballou attended Nichols Academy for six months in 1846 or

Monroe Nichols (1834–1867)
Educator, principal of Nichols Academy from 1857 to 1862.
Served in Civil War, captured and sent to notorious Libby Prison.
Died a few years after his release. Source: William C. Walker, History
of the *Eighteenth Regiment of Connecticut in the War for the Union*
(Norwich, Conn.: published by committee, 1885), facing page 14.

1847 and paid the ultimate price at the Battle of Bull Run on July 21, 1861.[17] Another was the popular Principal Monroe Nichols who enlisted in the 18th Connecticut Infantry in 1862. He was commissioned a captain, then taken prisoner at Winchester, Virginia, in fighting just before Gettysburg. Although later freed after a difficult time in Libby prison, he died shortly after the war. An incomplete and conservative projection suggests that at least fifteen former Academy students probably gave their lives in the American Civil War.[18]

But the horrors of war, the assassination of President Abraham Lincoln, and the turmoil of post-war peace and reconstruction all worked to energize a dramatically expanding American society. This was about to be a world quite different from pre-Civil War America with its unknown potential and unexplored horizons. Three cases provided by young men who attended Nichols Academy in the 1850s show the great range of choices available to aggressive and far reaching young Americans after 1865. That they had a Nichols Academy education was extremely helpful. The adventures of George Whitefield Davis, James Harvey Blood, and Hezekiah Conant, former Academy students, illustrate the depth and nature of the new world open to them after the American Civil War. Their careers differed significantly from those of earlier Nichols "scholars" – and from each other.

Major General George Whitefield Davis (1839–1918)
Nichols Academy student from Thompson, Conn. Engineer
and Major General in United States Army, served as assistant engineer
of Washington Monument construction. Military Governor of Puerto Rico
and involved in canal planning and management for Nicaraguan and
Panama Canal projects. Chairman, Central Committee of American
Red Cross. Courtesy American Red Cross.

George Whitefield Davis, a pre-war Academy student from Thompson, Connecticut, eventually became a major general in the United States Army after fighting in several major Civil War battles including Antietam. His later experiences as a representative of his country offer a picture of a growing American expansionism not conceivable before 1860. During his long military career, primarily as an engineer, Davis served in Arizona and New Mexico, became a key engineer in the construction of the Washington monument, was the first military governor of Puerto Rico, and became involved in the planning of a Nicaraguan Canal as well as the Panama Canal. He also commanded an Army Corps in the Philippine Islands and was assigned to Guatemala before his military retirement. Davis then served as chairman of the American Red Cross between 1907 and 1915.[19]

An even less traditional path, but just as revealing of the broadening new world, was taken by James Harvey Blood, a former Dudley resident and Academy student. Like Davis, Colonel Blood served in the Union Army in the Civil War. He emerged to become, according to one biased observer, "a radical of extreme radicalism – an internationalist of the most uncompromising type – a communist who would have rather died in Paris than be president of a

Colonel James Harvey Blood (1833–1885)
Academy student born in Dudley, Mass. Mentor and husband of
Victoria Woodhull, the first woman presidential candidate of
the U.S. Courtesy Victoria Woodhull & Company.

pretended republic. . . ."[20] These were strong words. Colonel Blood attended Nichols Academy in 1850, moving west with his family to St. Louis in 1857. During the Civil War, he was a colonel and commander of the 6th Missouri Infantry of the Union Army returning home to St. Louis with at least five bullet wounds. He then was elected city auditor of St. Louis and became president of the St. Louis Railroad, a company with horse-drawn cars. He also was the president of the local society of spiritualists.

Colonel Blood married Victoria Claflin Woodhull, best known as the first woman to run for president of the United States. They apparently were married and divorced at least twice between 1866 and 1876.[21] Nonetheless, Blood remained by Woodhull's side through thick and thin until 1875 or so.[22] According to accounts, the charming and well-educated Blood left his own family in St. Louis and went to New York with Woodhull and her family. He contributed much to her thinking about free love, spiritualism, women's suffrage, and labor exploitation. Considered a man of "a philosophical and reflective cast of mind," Colonel Blood wrote many of Woodhull's lectures, editorials and letters.[23]

He also managed the lucrative business opportunities of Woodhull's New York brokerage house and newspaper. His brother, George, who also had attended Nichols Academy, worked with them. Victoria Woodhull became an

Hezekiah Conant (1827–1902)
Builder of new Nichols Academy campus and Conant Memorial Church.
Born in Dudley, Mass., student at Nichols Academy from 1841–1845, 1850–1851.
Inventor, Rhode Island industrialist, member and president of the Nichols
Academy Board of Trustees. Source: Hezekiah Conant, *A Souvenir of the Conant
Memorial Church: Its Inception, Construction, and Dedication* (Boston: Forbes
Lithograph Manufacturing Company, 1893) opposite title page.

aggressive women's rights crusader and was the first woman to address a congressional committee. Among his other adventures, Colonel Blood was arrested with Woodhull for publishing an account of the infamous Beecher-Tilden scandal in her newspaper. This put them both in jail on an obscenity charge.[24] After Woodhull left for England, Blood relocated in Maine for a short time and then went to Ghana in Africa in search of gold. His search was successful, but he died of exhaustion following a number of cave-ins on the West Coast of Africa between Sierre Leone and Lagos in 1885. A colleague with him at the end saw James Harvey Blood as an "honest fellow." One of Victoria Woodhull's many biographers, Mary Gabriel, suggests that Woodhull must have had some feelings of remorse for the man "who had taught her so much."[25] As was the case with General Davis, Colonel Blood's experiences illuminate the expanding dimensions of a society unimaginable by the likes of Amasa Nichols or Hosea Ballou.

Certainly the travels and experiences of both General Davis and Colonel Blood present an extreme and revealing snapshot of a world in the making. In contrast, during this same period, Hezekiah Conant, a Dudley boy who attended the Academy the same year as James and George Blood, took advantage of the world Davis and Blood seemed to have left behind. In the years between 1860 and 1895, Conant used his exceptional inventive skills and organizational abilities to expand his fortune eventually building the largest thread mill in Rhode Island. This too was possible in the new world. He became a millionaire in the process. Eventually Conant made his skills and fortune available to Nichols Academy as will be noted later. While few matched the extent of this trio's combined range of experiences and successes in their wondrous new America, all Americans were touched by these same opportunities in one way or another. For Davis, Blood, and Conant, in large part, their opportunities had been made possible because of a Nichols Academy education.

While the fortunes of these former Academy students began to increase, Nichols Academy was facing a difficult time. As the Civil War progressed, enrollment numbers began to fall. By 1863, significant numbers of men were leaving to serve with the Union Army. Younger brothers and sisters replaced them on the farm and took still additional numbers away from the Academy. Understandably, public funds were being diverted to the war effort and unavailable for buildings and other expenses related to school construction. When the Nichols trustees discussed replacing the Academy building in the early 1860s, they found that a loan from the state was not possible because of increased government expenses "due to the rebellion."[26]

Somehow Academy building needs had to be met. By mid-1863, Academy trustees discussed the possibility of either purchasing the adjacent brick meeting house of the Universalist Society or constructing a "suitable" building on Academy grounds for $5,000.[27] After much discussion, Academy trustees approved the acquisition of the Universalist Meeting House in December 1867.[28] It was agreed that if this structure eventually had to be demolished, the proceeds would "be applied toward erecting a new building for the benefit of said institution."[29] At that point, the Academy owned two buildings on the town's main street for the first time in the Academy's history. They both needed extensive work.

Difficulties with its buildings coupled with fewer students meant lean years during the late 1860s. In 1869, the institution experienced three different principals and, with students "being so few," was forced to close in the middle of the year. The potential was such that no catalogue was published for several years.[30] Clearly many were concerned about its future. Nonetheless, by the spring of 1870, the *Webster Times* reported that Nichols Academy "still lives" and was to be open for the next term. Its survival, according to the *Times*, was a "most agreeable surprise."[31] Twenty-five students were enrolled for the next two terms.

Additional discussion by the Academy trustees then focused on putting rooms in the former Universalist Meeting House "for the better accommodation of the school."[32] Other recommendations included repairing the old academy building and constructing a new building with the second and third stories for students.[33] The Academy projected the total cost of working on three buildings to be $20,000, but they had no identifiable sources for these funds.

Raising money was not unknown to Academy supporters of the 1860s. Frequently, alternatives for fund raising were discussed by trustees in terms familiar to modern fund raisers. First, they considered obtaining subscriptions from townspeople since most families had sent one or more of its sons or daughters to the Academy. Second, a trustee committee recommended contacting everyone ever connected with the Academy to ask them "to remember their alma mater by sending the treasurer one dollar or more as they please." Third, they discussed applying to the town of Dudley for a "sum of money as shall be needed to complete the buildings." Then too, an Academy committee suggested festivals and lectures to raise additional sums although public lotteries generally had not worked for other academies. As a last resort, the Academy requested the state in 1869 to allow the town to raise a sum not exceeding $25,000, but was turned down when the town of Dudley apparently did not support this request. Clearly the Academy's future was in doubt at this point.[34]

"NICHOLS ACADEMY AND HIGH SCHOOL, DUDLEY, MASS."[35]

Nichols Academy was not alone in facing serious challenges at the beginning of the next decade. In 1870, the town of Dudley reviewed the ability of its public school system to assure compliance with state laws establishing high schools in Commonwealth communities. The Massachusetts Act of 1827 regarding secondary education in Massachusetts required that every town, city or district with over 500 families have a "master of good morals" to instruct the English branches [reading, writing, orthography, English grammar], geography, arithmetic, good behavior, the history of the United States, bookkeeping, geometry, surveying, and algebra and to "instruct a school" for at least ten months a year.[36] If the town of Dudley constructed a high school, the Academy would have been forced to close since Dudley students made up an increasing percentage of its struggling enrollment.

Free public high schools had been established in the neighboring communities of Webster, Oxford and Southbridge in the years between 1853 and 1856. Under the Act of 1827, state oversight of Massachusetts education was provided by a state board of education. Horace Mann, the first Massachusetts secretary of education in 1837, believed it was the responsibility of the state to support and direct public education.[37] Academies were not part of Mann's design. As he saw it, private academies separated better-prepared students from the ranks of those attending public high school thereby lowering the overall quality of public schools. Furthermore, academies simply did not conform to the republican model being promoted by Mann and the state. To add to the discussion, approximately 70 percent of Massachusetts citizens lived in towns with public high schools by 1865.[38]

While this was occurring, the Nichols Academy trustees had to reconsider their Academy building that was fifty years old. They remarked that the structure had been remodeled and repaired so often that it was similar to a boy's jackknife "that had three new handles and five new blades but was the same old knife."[39] Their recommendation called for repairing the building, although there was little agreement as to how much they could afford. When the Academy trustees turned again for assistance from the town of Dudley after cancelling the winter term in 1869–1870, the institution could not have been in worse shape.[40]

Nichols Academy was saved in 1871 by an agreement with Dudley. This same agreement greatly assisted the town as well by allowing it to avoid the expense of constructing and staffing a new high school. According to the 1870 United States census, Dudley had grown to 485 families, or almost to the 500 families designated by the state as requiring that a local high school be constructed.[41] The next year, the town meeting of Dudley voted 114 to 84 to give the Academy $12,000 in six annual payments to assist in "repairing and rebuilding" Academy buildings. It also agreed to pay $1,000 annually to the Academy for furnishing instruction "in those branches required to be taught in high school" for all children in Dudley qualified to enter the Academy in both lower and upper high school grades.[42] Dudley now had its high school. Dudley high school students could take the same courses at Nichols Academy as those students from other locations.[43] The Nichols Academy Board of Trustees also agreed that if the Academy failed to furnish high school instruction, the town could use the brick school house (formerly the Universalist Meeting House) as a high school.[44]

Academy trustees immediately accepted the town vote.[45] Importantly, the town now had its high school and the ability to satisfy state requirements while providing its students with a secondary school education from a well-known school.[46] Nichols Academy had secured its immediate future as well. Thirty-five Dudley students then enrolled in the Academy for the next term beginning August 21, 1871.[47]

The Academy quickly began to change. The former brick meeting house was repaired and readied for use as the Academy school house at a cost of nearly $4,000.[48] The trustees then rejected doing anything more with the old

Fig. 4.1. Grade Report for Nichols Academy/Dudley High School Student, June 19, 1896

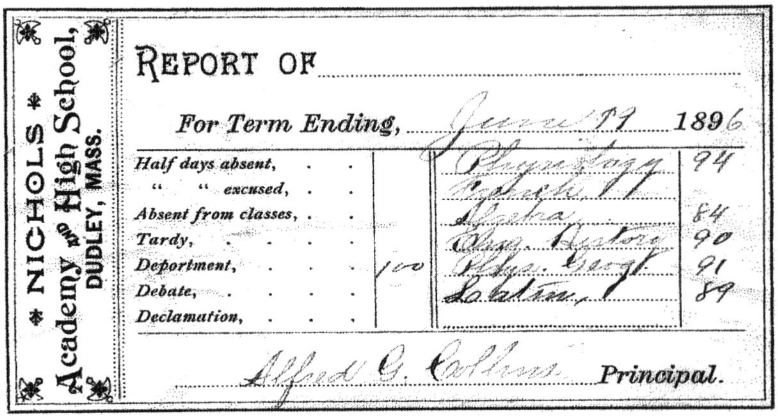

* NICHOLS *
Academy AND High School,
DUDLEY, MASS.

REPORT OF

For Term Ending, June 19 1896

Half days absent,			94
" " excused,			
Absent from classes,		Algebra	84
Tardy,		Gen. History	90
Deportment,	100	Phys. Geog.	91
Debate,		Latin	89
Declamation,			

Alfred G. Collins **Principal.**

Source: Folder #19, NCA.

Academy building and made plans to construct a new boarding house. In their meeting on September 26, 1873, they reported that a boarding house with two stories and an attic containing a total of twenty-rooms was completed at a cost of $8,380.[49] The old Academy building originally built by Amasa Nichols was then razed in 1873.[50] (See Nichols Academy campus, ca. 1878, page 8.) In an effort to fund yet another structure, they went back to the legislature for $25,000, but this effort failed as before.[51] Nonetheless, the shaky Academy was in partnership with the town of Dudley and both were able to look ahead. A new Academy was about to emerge. Ten years after the 1871 agreement, the town of Dudley reported that "Nichols Academy constitutes the Town High School and forms a very important future in our local system of education."[52] (See Fig. 4.1.)

THE GREAT DEBATE: PUBLIC EDUCATION OR THE ACADEMY WAY

Secondary education in Massachusetts during the immediate post-Civil War years was the subject of a critical debate with far-reaching consequences. Supporters of academies were being challenged by citizens and state officials alike who believed in a free public school system supported and controlled by state government. The academy or "rural" way was being challenged by the perceived needs of an industrial society, increasing immigration, and continuing efforts to achieve greater democracy. The dictates of an increasingly powerful state educational system were promoting this change.

Academies had developed early detractors despite their successes. There were many Americans who had not supported the actions and thinking that promoted private academies. Some feared that academies might convince their children to stay away from farm work.[53] Interestingly, this concern could be applied to farmers' daughters as well as to their sons. For instance, northern New England farmers suffered greatly in the 1830s and 1840s when their daughters left for Lowell, Massachusetts, to work in the textile factories. One journal, the *Farmer's Monthly Visitor*, bemoaned the fact that "good dairy-women are becoming more and more scarce." It then asked "If not to the rising fair generation, to whom shall we look for the hands that are to supply so important a portion of subsistence as the product of the dairy?"[54]

While many Lowell and Nichols Academy young women eventually returned home, some did not. The Academy and the factory were similar in that the impact of the loss of a contributing family member was the same. For instance, in a later day, Mary Bair of Dudley, who attended classes at the High School at Dudley Hill, was told by her mother, that she was not to milk the cows. This would have tied her to the day-to-day routine of the farm. "If you learn to milk the cows, you always will milk the cows" was the way it was put. Mary Bair followed this advice. She did everything else on the farm, but she did not milk the cows. After graduating from Bartlett High School in Webster, and Bridgewater Normal School, she became a school library director in Quincy, Massachusetts.[55] The possibility that hands – male and female – could be lost was a terrifying thought to long established family farms.

Others resented the control of academies sometimes exercised by town elite in village centers. In many cases, as had occurred at Nichols Academy between 1819 and 1823, the leaders of academies were not intended to be local – by design. Some academy constitutions had carefully spelled out the composition of their boards of trustees. And, if significant religious, social, and cultural differences existed in these communities, even greater suspicions and antagonisms arose. Not surprisingly, battle lines were clearly drawn between the positions of the Massachusetts Board of Education and academies in the state by the 1860s, if not earlier.

Free public high schools were applauded by the state and its supporters who condemned the academy way. As they saw it, a state or national educational system was the logical means to achieve the unification of the power and ideological content of republicanism with the value structure of Protestantism. According to Henry Barnard, the first Connecticut commissioner of common schools and later the first United States commissioner of education, national education was "at once a cause and an effect of the national character."[56] Horace Mann's earlier work as secretary of the board of education in Massachusetts had preceded Barnard by a few years.

Not surprisingly, they held similar positions regarding the direction of American education.

As Horace Mann saw it, the relatively small number of academies in Massachusetts could not provide adequate educational leadership for a rapidly expanding industrial society. A state department with educators working for the good of the state and its citizens was the answer for Mann and his supporters.[57] He wanted schooling that was more common, more equal, and completely directed by public policy.[58] His common school was to be public, free to students, and run by elected public officials.[59] The private and seemingly elitist independent academy did not fit this mold.

Not surprisingly, academies responded aggressively. Many academy supporters believed that the public would not back secondary education as Mann expected. Some felt that secondary education was a luxury only for those who could afford it. Others simply thought that many young Americans were not capable of benefiting from secondary education and the taxpayer should not have to pay for their education. Some accepted the idea of spending public money for education, but felt it was better handled by private interests such as academies. Many distrusted the abilities of new public high schools to develop long-term public support for education. They thought public schools might begin enthusiastically, but that strife and bickering would disrupt the work of these schools. Still others believed that academies simply provided better educational opportunities.[60]

A significant number of supporters also pointed to the past successes experienced by academies. After all, much had been accomplished by academies between 1780 and 1860. When the Reverend Calvin D. Hulbert, then president of Middlebury College, addressed a celebration of Barre Academy in Vermont in 1877, he presented a number of strong points on which he built his argument for the permanence of the academy "way." He stated that academies were located at convenient locations resulting in no additional expenses. He, too, was concerned about the moral climate in larger communities, but, unlike the anti-academy people, he was certain that academy's environment placed students with similar classmates in a location where they could do their best studying. Moral challenges in an academy environment were fewer, as he saw it. Rural locations created an important sense of independence for the individual. Hulbert felt that the academy was a community. He believed that the strong religious and moral foundations developed in most academies were positive forces necessary to counterbalance the commercial and secular tendencies then permeating New England society.[61]

Nichols Academy was caught in the conflict that radiated from this "great debate." With its own immediate problems seemingly under control by 1880 thanks to the town and Hezekiah Conant, it was possible for John R. Thayer, a

Nichols Academy trustee, to comment on the future relationship between the state and the academy. A former Nichols Academy student and Yale graduate, now a state representative and soon-to-be a member of the U.S. House of Representatives, Thayer eloquently expressed his reasons for supporting the "old academy":

> . . . no [educational] system however perfect can meet the demands and satisfy the wants of crowded cities and large towns and at the same time accommodate the small outlying towns and sparsely populated districts. In these latter places the people still cling to the district schools and the old academies and their usefulness remains unquestioned and the demand for their continuance unabating; and I predict that in the not far distant future the present educational system of the state will be so far modified and changed so as to permit those sparsely settled districts to waive the provisions for high schools and contribute to the maintenance of the old academies. . . . [62]

Thayer's assessments regarding the past and the present were accurate. Former Nichols principal, Marcellus Coggan, echoed Thayer several years later.[63] Unfortunately, their vision for the future was not accurate. As sensitive and well-meaning as Thayer and Coggan may have been, they simply misjudged the force of democracy as well as the power and determination of the state board of education. They also overlooked the cultural diversity emerging in Dudley as young mill operatives began to outnumber farm workers and foreign-born residents prepared to gain a voice in town politics.[64]

The "Second Founder": Hezekiah Conant[65]

When Trustee John Thayer referred in 1881 to the Academy as "This Grand Old Institution of Learning," he was speaking about an institution that no longer existed.[66] The former Universalist Meeting House had been renovated with funds provided by the town. By 1867, it was serving as the Academy school house and was to last until 1881. The older building built by Amasa Nichols and once the heart and soul of the Academy had been torn down by 1873.

Old Nichols Academy had never been what is frequently referred to as a boarding school; this phenomenon had just begun to appear in the latter half of the nineteenth century. When the new boarding house of Nichols Academy set slightly to the northwest of the old Academy building was completed and first used in 1873, it was ready to house fifty-five students.[67] The decision to construct a formal dwelling house, as they called it, had been discussed at length in trustee meetings. Nonetheless, there were specific issues regarding such a building. Some argued that greater control over their students was necessary since American society itself was becoming more diverse. Others felt

85

that a substantial boarding house gave the Academy a clear advantage over institutions that did not have them. However, this development weakened the structure of the learning village which had been the product of like value systems. And, in part due to this complex learning relationship, Nichols Academy had been a point of local pride as well as a center of regional education.

Following the Academy-Dudley agreement in 1871, the arrival of Hezekiah Conant on the Academy board of trustees in 1874 was the second monumental event of the 1870s. The earlier agreement with the town made it possible for the Academy to remain open. Conant then brought commitment, leadership, a much needed force of character, and impressive financial support. He was a direct descendant (eighth generation) of Roger Conant who settled in the Plymouth Colony in 1623 and then in Salem in 1626. Roger Conant sometimes is referred to as the first leader of the colony that later became Massachusetts Bay. Hezekiah Conant's great grandfather, Josiah, arrived in the northern part of Dudley in the 1750s settling near Baker Pond. Hezekiah's father, Hervey Conant, owned a farm and operated a grist mill that he eventually sold to woolen manufacturer Aaron Tufts.

Hezekiah Conant was born in 1827. His first years were spent as a child in somewhat above average rural conditions. Similar to most young people in rural Dudley, Hezekiah's early years saw him helping his father on their farm. At six, he attended a district elementary school on the road from Tufts village to Dudley Center (later called Ramshorn Road), probably during the winter months.[68] At the age of fourteen in 1841, he began at Nichols Academy attending at least one term each year until 1845 when he moved to nearby Worcester, Massachusetts. Then 18, he worked there for a brief time as a roller boy in the printing offices of the *Worcester County Gazette* and the *National Aegis*. He next worked a year in a machine shop saving enough money to pay for additional terms at Nichols Academy in 1850 and 1851. Now 23, Conant returned to Worcester and the machine shop, taking time in the evening to study mechanical drawing and mechanical engineering.

In the fifteen years after Conant left Nichols Academy, his mechanical expertise was put to good use in three states and a number of different manufacturing environments. This was an unparalleled time for inventors, makers of tools – actually of all things mechanical. Moreover, the American industrial revolution presented additional and even greater opportunities for those who also could organize work. Hezekiah Conant could invent and he could organize patterns of work. After his second stay at the Academy, Conant worked in the locomotive shop of the Union works in South Boston and for the Sharpe Rifle Company. He also worked for S. Slater & Co. in Webster, Massachusetts, before going to Willimantic, Connecticut, where he developed machinery for handling thread and spools including a ticketing machine for labeling spools.

From Connecticut, he moved to Pawtucket, Rhode Island, where, in 1868, at the age of 41, he organized the Conant Thread Company. Operating as its treasurer and manager, he became associated with J. & P. Coats of Paisley, Scotland, and increased the number of his workers to 3,000.[69] His inventions – he held as many as thirteen patents – were in categories as diverse as clocks, thread winding, firearms, boots, sprinklers, looms, paper, and casting projectiles. Conant also developed a process of knurling spools of thread (embossing the size number of the thread on the edge of each spool) and made improvements in spool winding machines for his thread company. His greatest entrepreneurial success probably was in building and managing the largest thread mill in Rhode Island.[70] Well on his way to becoming a millionaire, Hezekiah Conant joined the Nichols Academy Board of Trustees in 1874.

There can be little question that Hezekiah Conant had remained in contact with his old town and his former academy. For one thing, his first two wives, Sarah Williams and Harriet Knight Learned (he was married three times), were sisters who came from Dudley. He greatly regretted that the town of Dudley was not the same community he had left thirty years before. Time had clearly lessened the importance of Dudley Hill. The Academy also was not the same. However, one important factor of continuity in the Academy's history did exist. The Academy's board of trustees had been controlled by Dudley trustees since 1823 and this was to continue with Hezekiah Conant now its leader.

A large section of the town of Dudley had been cut away in 1832 to create the town of Webster. The new town received desirable land and water rights along the French River and Webster Lake. This action was based on the request by Samuel Slater and his family to the state legislature to allow the Slaters and their companies to provide better services to the eastern part of old Dudley. The town of Oxford to the north suffered no less than Dudley as it also lost land and productive citizens to the new town to be named after Daniel Webster. Angry Dudley voters voiced a strong objection in 1831 rejecting the Slater-sponsored petition for a new town. They believed the creation of this new town "would be manifestly injurious and unjust."[71] The Massachusetts legislature saw the issue differently and apparently was impressed by the achievements of Samuel Slater skillfully presented by his attorney, Daniel Webster. This decision resulted in the loss of one-fifth of Dudley's territory, one-third of its population, and one quarter of its rateable property. It would be difficult to recover from this loss.[72]

Voters in Dudley complained that two-thirds of the new community of Webster was in the service of the Slater mills and dependent on the Slaters. For many Dudley voters, Samuel Slater was seen as having too much power for "one man under a free government."[73] Webster was quickly incorporated and became a growing mill town with a railroad after 1836. While it is easy to blame Samuel Slater for Dudley's problems that followed, an industrial revolution was occurring that was to bring social and economic change, regardless of the details.

Dudley's slow subsequent growth reflected this loss of land. Between 1810 and 1830, its population had expanded from 1,226 to 2,155. Ten years later it was down to 1,452.[74] It took sixty more years for Dudley's population to reach 2,742.[75] When it did expand, the town's population center had moved "downhill" away from the village of Dudley Hill or Dudley Center and to the east and the French River. Across the river on former Dudley land, Webster was rapidly growing as a manufacturing community and a significant commercial center with the Norwich and Worcester Railroad bringing additional prosperity to the town built by the Slater family. Dudley Hill was not the population or commercial center of Dudley when Hezekiah Conant returned to his old school.

Conant's account of the Dudley Hill he knew as a boy suggests how much the former center of Dudley had changed in his eyes. His somewhat idyllic view nonetheless reflected a common sense of loss experienced by many late nineteenth century rural Americans. His recollection of old Dudley Hill was included in an address to the annual graduation and ninth reunion class of Nichols Academy in 1883. In his words:

> I can remember when Dudley [Hill] was a busy place where there were two stores, and they were not limited to dry goods exclusively; they dealt in West India goods and hardware. Saloons were not invented then, but the two aforesaid were saloons, they were banks of discount, they were the brokers' board, the board of trade, the produce exchange, the military and police headquarters. Then there was a hotel which stood across the street [from the new Academy building] which was pro bono publico, and entertained man and beast; the Boston & Hartford stage carrying the U. S. Mail stopped there and fed its passengers and changed horses, and rolled away down the hill with its noise and dust. We had military companies, we had two blacksmith shops, we had Mark Elwell's furniture factory, we had a hat factory, and eclipsing them all was the "horn" or Tufts woolen factory away up north where Captain Conant's grist and saw mills used to be. We used to have musters of military, artillery and cavalry exhibitions on the Glorious Fourth. But while all the rest of the country has been thriving and fattening on the progress of manufactures, agriculture and commerce, this town gradually failed, till now it is like [Oliver] Goldsmith's "Deserted Village," and the very spot where everything above related is forgot, perhaps, excepting this old Nichols Academy. . . .[76]

Whereas Goldsmith's "Deserted Village" had resulted from the agricultural revolution in England and Ireland, the decline of the village of Dudley Hill was seen by Conant as caused by an industrial revolution that passed it by. Ironically, the same forces that made Conant a wealthy man had led to Dudley Hill's decline as a commercial center. Although old Dudley Hill had "failed" in Conant's eyes, he was determined that the Academy was not going to experience a similar fate. To avoid this possibility, he rebuilt and reshaped the Nichols Academy campus and, eventually, the top of Dudley Hill.

There is no indication that Hezekiah Conant had a solid vision of what he wanted to accomplish when he joined the Academy Board of Trustees in 1874.[77] Regardless, in the ten-year period between 1875 and 1885, he constructed an entirely new academy and its campus. In addition, in 1891 and 1893, he rebuilt the Congregational Church and assisted in constructing the town's new Center School.

When Conant became an Academy trustee, his old school had two functioning buildings: the former Universalist Meeting House just converted to a school house and a new boarding house (sometimes known as the Dwelling House) completed in 1873. Upon his arrival, the Academy mortgaged this property to him for $4,000.[78] His next step in reconstructing the campus was to rebuild the top of Dudley Hill by constructing a plateau extending for nearly two hundred yards to the west of the main street (or Center Road) and down Healy Road. Conant purchased more than an acre of land behind the Academy school house (former Universalist Meeting House) for "a common or play ground" or, if necessary, for one or more buildings "to be used for educational purposes in connection with said Academy as an institution of learning."[79] He then built a retaining wall three hundred feet long and twelve feet high that held back thousands of truckloads of fill dumped near the western boundary of Academy land.[80]

This was just the beginning. Now unhappy with the condition and placement of the old brick school house (the former Universalist Meeting House) on his newly constructed campus, Conant considered taking it down and reassembling it a short distance away. However, for this to be done, the Academy had to close for nearly a year. In April 1880 he asked the town to permit such a move; the voters agreed – and gave him $500 toward the project.[81] Changing his mind, in June that year, Conant erected a new Academy building which he completed in 1881.[82]

Constructed one hundred feet to the west of the Academy school house (former Universalist Meeting House), his Academy building became the new "school house." Trimmed with Longmeadow (Mass.) limestone and built with 160,000 bricks, it was 88 feet by 61 feet with a 76 foot tower and cost $13,000.[83]

This building was constructed by E. B. Durkee, a Dudley builder. An irregular structure of gothic design, Conant's Academy building contained "large and pleasant recitation rooms" including one school room 40 feet by 30 feet, two smaller recitation rooms 15 feet by 18 feet, and an exhibition room 51 feet by 40 feet with a stage, later named Alumni Hall, and capable of seating 500 people. In addition, there was a well-lighted basement to be used as a gymnasium."[84] Conant's wish was that the Alumni Hall, the building's largest room, would "always be used by the community."[85] He employed a nationally known Worcester architectural firm, Elbridge Boyden and Son, for this and for the next two buildings he was to build for the Academy. (For Conant's buildings, see Nichols Campus, page 9.)

On June 17, 1881, the land and the Academy building were conveyed to the trustees of the Academy by Conant. He then remarked about his gift:

> I take great pleasure in doing this on behalf of my native town, for the benefit of the old academy where I was educated; and if by my sacrifice of money and time for this purpose will encourage the boys of Dudley to be more faithful to their studies, to live an honest, useful life, to establish for themselves a character beloved at home and honored abroad, then I shall feel that I have made a good and satisfactory investment and that I have accomplished a good purpose.[86]

Transferred for "good will and other valuable considerations," to the Academy, his new building was then included in the Academy's 1871 agreement with the town.[87]

Conant's work was emphatically supported by the Dudley community. As a *Webster Times* reporter concluded, he was the person "to whom the people are indebted so much for this munificent gift [the Academy building] as well as for other and numerous evidences of generosity and affectionate regard for the lovely old hill-town. . . ."[88] This affection for Conant helps to explain why Dudley voters placed Civil War Memorial Tablets in the Academy Hall when it was dedicated. These tablets were the greatest gifts – the names of family members and friends who died in the American Civil War – that the people of Dudley could give to a gracious benefactor. These tablets acknowledged an important educational partnership and documented a community's friendship.

Plans for a second structure also were revealed in June 1881 when the Academy building was dedicated. Hezekiah Conant's compensation for the Academy building was the "material of the old building [the former Universalist Meeting House]" which he immediately decided to use for another structure: a library and observatory.[89] This was to be a "small building" about sixty feet south of the new Academy building intended for the scholars of the Academy as well as for the townspeople.[90] It was furnished with instruments of both astronomical and meteorological importance. These included "a large reflecting telescope of the best English make, with equational mountings . . . specially adapted for astronomical purposes." His meteorological instruments later included self-registering barometers, thermometers, and wind and rain gauges from instrument makers such as Cosella & Co. of London and Draper Company of New York.[91] The building itself was 27 feet by 40 feet with reading rooms and a tower 27 feet high.[92] He eventually deeded Conant Library and Observatory to the Academy in 1900 along with the boarding house he was to build in 1885.[93]

There is no question that the Conant Library and Observatory, while not large compared to the other two buildings Conant also built for the school, best captured the spirit of Conant's era. Although small, it was not a simple structure. Aside from a library that started with 600 books and quickly expanded to 2,000 volumes, it contained several other significant features that made it out-of-the-ordinary. First, the observatory was described as "the best equipped of any in New England outside of the colleges, and affords the fullest opportunity for practical work."[94] This structure included a reading room, space for a volunteer United States Signal Corps station, a telegraph, and a tower for the telescopes. A celestial and terrestrial telescope with a four and a half inch aperture made by Alvan Clark & Son of Cambridge, Mass., was added to the observatory as a gift to Conant from James Coats of Paisley, Scotland, and Providence, Rhode Island, in 1884 or 1885.[95]

Conant then located a transit house next to Conant Library and Observatory. This wooden structure, no more than ten feet by ten feet, was to cover a granite stone with a deep and carefully structured base. This stone, standing four feet above the ground, was the platform for a transit telescope. The transit house contained a slit through the roof through which the stars could be carefully observed. According to the Reverend Charles L. Goodell of Dudley, this building was taken down in the 1920s.[96]

Astronomy was most important for Conant. He believed everyone should be interested in the heavens. He also felt that meteorological changes – the force and speed of wind, rainfall amounts, atmospheric changes and ranges of temperature – were important to understand and to record. His little building was established as a volunteer U. S. Signal Corps Station with telegraphic communication to the outside world over Western Union lines.[97] Daily reports were sent to the Weather Bureau in Washington, D. C., from volunteers at Conant Library. According to one observer, the transit instrument and the chronographer both were made by Fauthe & Co., of Washington, D. C., and put in position on July 4, 1888.[98] The date was not a coincidence.

Conant's achievement in creating his library and observatory was crowned by another of his singularly impressive accomplishments. Consistent with his interests in astronomy and meteorology, he designed and patented a unique and stately "new and improved" Astronomical Clock which he placed in his library and observatory. In his request for a patent in 1887, he said: "The object of my invention is to provide a new and improved astronomical time-keeping instrument indicating the correct solar and sidereal time, and the right ascension of the mean sun."[99] A masterpiece, it is a ten-foot high duplex differential mechanical instrument that worked with his transit instrument in the transit house. This clock, one of three built for him by E. Howard & Co., has received numerous accolades from generations of clock makers.[100]

After describing the beginning of the library and observatory, Conant reflected briefly on the meaning of his work. He told Nichols Academy graduates in 1882 that the ". . . old institution, which has glimmered with wavering and struggling beams for the last sixty years, may glow with these new aids into a stronger and more steady light, so that people more remote shall behold and rejoice and be greatly benefitted thereby."[101]

Conant's final significant contribution to the Academy's campus came in 1885. Like the others, it had not been anticipated. Before Conant joined the Nichols Academy Board of Trustees, the Academy had constructed a new boarding house. This new boarding house, an imposing three-story wooden structure, was destroyed by fire in 1883 just after the Conant Library and Observatory building had been completed. Confronted with another challenge, Conant responded as before. He erected a new, brick boarding house that was ready for use in September 1885 at a cost of nearly $15,000. It was located on the site of the previous boarding house which had stood just to the north of the new Academy building.

Also designed by Elbridge Boyden and Son, the Conant-financed boarding house was named Roger Conant Hall and known as the Dudley Inn. This structure contained a dining hall and kitchen in its basement, suites for the preceptor and steward on the first floor, with at least ten sleeping rooms on each of the upper two floors for student boarders. One description pictured every room "fitted with an open fire place, giving it a cheerful and comfortable look." During the summer, the Dudley Inn was open to visitors interested in "a healthful and cool retreat from the city in the most delightful hill town where all the charms of outward nature may be used to advantage."[102] The next summer, ground was broken for a new brick barn behind the boarding house and hotel. As the *Webster Times* put it, "Mr. Conant is as usual the man who backs this job."[103]

In short, the Academy's facilities were totally rebuilt between 1877 and 1885. The Conant-designed and financed campus rejuvenated the little school by providing an essentially modern physical plant composed of three small to medium-sized buildings. There was, however, more to institution-making than new buildings, telescopes, and clocks. It would take time before the success of Conant and his architects could be determined. There was nothing mysterious about the financial condition of the Academy before 1880. Trustee Thayer said that there had been times when the Academy's "life pulse beat low, and her best friends were anxious lest the end was near." All evidence suggests he was right.[104]

Although the "end" was avoided, many problems still existed. In 1882, Trustee Thayer believed that "the chief need now is for more students . . . ." and he urged everyone to "secure one hundred students" for the next school year.[105] Two years later, Trustee Clark Jillson acknowledged Hezekiah Conant's earlier comment that the Academy "never was in better condition than today," but agreed with Thayer regarding the need for more students.[106] Conant had constructed the buildings necessary for a new academy. He had transformed his former home town and the Hill. However, there was much to be done if this new academy was to emerge from under the pile of rubble that had been Amasa Nichols' old Academy building.

CHAPTER 5

THE NATURE OF MR. CONANT'S ACADEMY, 1874~1902

Hezekiah Conant's munificence gave the Academy both the ability and the mandate to advance into the twentieth century. This does not suggest that success was assured. Those responsible for the Academy's course had difficult decisions due to changing educational needs necessarily coupled with new pedagogical and cultural shifts. Nichols Academy trustees consistently pointed to the Academy's need for students although the growing Dudley public school system added to its enrollment.

While the Nichols campus was being methodically reconstructed by the wealthy and determined Hezekiah Conant, its mission was being defined and directed as much by its past as it was by careful thinking about the future. With the assistance of three financial aid funds (the Hancock, Congdon, and Conant Funds) and tuition agreements with the towns of Dudley and Charlton, short-term institutional income was not a problem – as long as Dudley students came to Dudley Hill and Hezekiah Conant supported the Academy.

After 1875, Nichols Academy trustees and principals faced specific challenges. They had to consider critical issues such as the nature of the Academy itself, the possibility of an eventual closing, the chance that the Academy building could belong to the town of Dudley, and the potential the school offered to become a different institution.[1] While Hezekiah Conant rebuilt the Academy buildings, he worked with its trustees and principals attempting to place the school's academic program on a competitive and viable footing.[2] This was a necessary first step. They adjusted the curriculum by "modernizing" courses and eventually merged long-held purposes.[3] In the process, they had to consider both the needs of a rural mill town high school and those of a college preparatory school interested in "fitting" students for the best colleges and universities in the northeast. This was a difficult challenge for a small rural academy.

A New Purpose and Program

No matter the contributions of rural academies in Massachusetts prior to the American Civil War, the post-war educational environment required significant adjustments. Public schools grew rapidly in number during this period. By 1876, more than 190 public high schools existed in Massachusetts as opposed to 57 academies. More than two-thirds of Massachusetts public schools offered the same English programs found in academies and one-third provided college preparatory programs.[4]

Other adjustments were necessary as well. For instance, prior to the Civil War, colleges and universities had granted admission based on a prospective student's performance on entrance interviews and examinations. By the mid 1870s, colleges were formalizing their entrance requirements resulting in the need for secondary schools to be more responsive to college admission directives. Furthermore, beginning with the last decades of the nineteenth century, accrediting agencies were establishing specific guidelines for higher education.[5] A process of educational standardization had begun.

These developments affected the program and approach of Nichols Academy, as well as other similar schools. By 1873, Nichols Academy announced its intention to work closely with its scholars who were "intending to fit themselves for our higher institutions of learning."[6] Three years later, the Academy referred to its "College Fitting Department" as the "distinctive one of the Academy." Graduates of what was then a three-year Academy program were said to be qualified to take "enviable positions in the first colleges in the country." Similarly, notices were placed in publications such as the *Boston University Beacon* recognizing Nichols Academy as a "First-Class Fitting School" with its students being "fitted for Boston University, Harvard and Yale."[7] The Academy now referred to itself as a "Preparatory School," while also operating as the town's high school.[8] In essence, it served two masters.

Continued emphasis on the Academy's college "fitting" program logically caused its focus to shift. Nichols Academy Catalogues began to list recent graduates of the Academy and the colleges they attended. These institutions, and the number of Nichols students in attendance between 1879 and 1890, included: Boston University (3), Harvard (1), Amherst (4), Williams (6), Dartmouth (1), Bowdoin (1), state (Massachusetts) normal school (3), Bates (1), Sheffield Scientific – Yale (1), and Boston Medical University (2).[9] According to Academy Catalogues, the Academy's Classical course, the primary program for college preparation, was increased to a four-year program, and "designed to fit thoroughly for any of our American Colleges. . . ."[10]

Three basic courses were featured in the Academy's curriculum in 1873: the Classical or college preparatory course; an Academic course "for those not going to pursue higher courses of study;" and a course for students interested in becoming teachers.[11] These curriculum objectives were refined ten years later after the Academy dropped any reference to a course for teachers when state normal schools became solidly established. One program was a complete preparation for college and the other for those with business interests. Dudley High School students could select either program. It is important to note that the Academy considered these programs equal in both mental training and focus on culture.[12]

Within a few years, the Academy recognized an increasing interest in science by adding a Literary and Scientific course of study featuring mathematics, the natural sciences, English language, and literature. It was designed to assist admission to an increasing number of technical colleges although it did not replace the Classical course. This was done with the encouragement of Hezekiah Conant. The Commercial course continued as a "faithful" preparation for business featuring, among other subjects, bookkeeping, commercial penmanship, arithmetic, and commercial law.[13] The Academy considered this course "equal to that offered by the best business colleges. . . ."[14] In effect, the Academy's dual curriculum was broadened to include a third course or program. (See Fig. 5.1.)

In the process of improving its course offerings, the Academy utilized Hezekiah Conant's library and observatory. After his new buildings had been completed in 1881 and 1882, Academy announcements spelled out that the Literary and Scientific course was for those "whose minds naturally turn to scientific investigation. . . ."[15] Hezekiah Conant, who later became president of the Nichols Academy Board of Trustees, clearly supported this new program. He commented:

> I wish to state that in the coming year we propose to be able to give instruction in mechanical and freehand drawing and in surveying and civil engineering work and environmental chemistry and also practical astronomy.[16]

Conant admitted that this program was a "pet scheme" of his own, although similar programs did exist in a few other academies.

Over the next ten years, the Literary and Scientific course graduated the largest number of Nichols scholars. At the same time, the general curriculum expanded to include subjects such as telegraphy (a diploma-granting course), civil engineering, and commercial penmanship.[17] The telegraph station in the Conant Library and Observatory was supervised by an experienced operator and provided "unusual facilities for learning telegraphy."[18] This was the type of academy that Mr. Conant appreciated.

Along with an expanded academic offering, the Academy also substantially improved its extra-curricular program and recognized the institution's greater role in student health and exercise. In early America, life on the farm had

Fig. 5.1. Nichols Academy Courses of Study, 1896

LITERARY AND SCIENTIFIC COURSE OF STUDY

First Year

Fall Term	*Winter Term*	*Spring Term*
Algebra 5	Algebra 5	Algebra 5
Physical Geography 2	Physical Geography 2	Physical Geography 2
English History 3	English History 3	English History 3
Commercial Arithmetic 3	Commercial Arithmetic 2	Commercial Arithmetic 2
Higher English 3	Higher English 3	Higher English 3
Latin, French or German 5	Latin, French or German 5	Latin, French ,German 5

Second Year

Physiology 2	Physiology 2	Physiology 2
University Algebra 3	University Algebra 3	University Algebra 3
Botany 2	Botany 2	Botany 2
Physics 3	Physics 3	Physics 3
Book-keeping *5	Book-keeping *5	Book-keeping *5
Rhetoric 5	Rhetoric 5	Rhetoric 5
Latin, French or German 5	Latin, French or German 5	Latin, French, German 5

Third Year

Geometry 5	Geometry 5	Geometry 5
Drawing 2	Drawing 2	Drawing 2
Chemistry 3	Chemistry 3	Chemistry 3
Geology 2	Geology 2	Geology 2
General History 3	General History 5	General History 5
Latin, French or German 5	Latin, French or German 5	Latin, French, German 5

Fourth Year

Civil Government 2	Civil Government 2	Civil Government 2
Solid Geometry 3	S. Geometry or Trig. 5	S. Geom. or Surveying 3
Political Economy 2	Political Economy 2	Political Economy 2
Astronomy 3	Astronomy 3	Astronomy 3
Ethics 2	Ethics 2	Ethics 2
Psychology 3	Psychology 3	Psychology 3
English Literature 5	English Literature 5	English Literature 5
Latin, French or German 5	Latin, French or German 5	Latin, French, German 5

Expression, Stenography, Typewriting and Physical Culture every day throughout the course.
Numbers after subjects denote the number of recitations per week.
*Optional.

CLASSICAL COURSE

First Year

Fall Term	*Winter Term*	*Spring Term*
Latin Lessons	Latin Grammar	Latin Composition
Latin Grammar	Misc. Latin Grammar	Cæsar
Latin Reader	Algebra	Algebra
Algebra	English History	Roman History
English History		Greek History

Declamation and Composition throughout the year.

Second Year

Latin Composition	Latin Composition	Latin Composition
Cæsar	Virgil	Virgil
Greek Grammar	Greek Grammar	Anabasis
Geometry	Geometry	Grecian History
Greek Lessons	Greek Lessons	Greek Lessons

Declamation and Composition throughout the year.

Third Year

Latin Composition	Latin Composition	Latin Composition
Virgil	Cicero	Cicero and Ovid
Anabasis	Anabasis	Iliad or Anabasis
French	French	French
Greek Composition	Ovid	Geometry
	Greek Composition	Greek Composition

Fourth Year

Virgil	Virgil	Review in Math.
Iliad	Iliad	Latin Review
German	Odyssey	French and German
Greek Composition	French and German	French
Latin Composition		German
Original Orations throughout the year.		Roman History

COMMERCIAL COURSE

". . . Thorough instruction in bookkeeping by double entry, Commercial Penmanship, Arithmetic. Commercial Law, Telegraphy. This course is equal to that offered by the best business colleges with the added benefits of wholesome discipline and careful supervision. . . . The telegraph station in the Observatory, with a skillful operator, affords unusual facilities for learning telegraphy."

Source: *Annual Catalogue . . . Nichols Academy. . . 1896* (Pawtucket, R.I.: Adam Sutcliffe Co., 1896), 14-21, NCA.

provided sufficient regular physical exercise for most Americans. This was changing by the Civil War as rural and agrarian America moved farther west. As a result, exercise or fitness programs and gymnastics appeared in many schools soon to be followed by organized sports. By 1880, Nichols Academy had added daily light gymnastics sessions in the Academy Hall that involved the whole school in exercises featuring dumb bells or four-foot wands sometimes done to music.[19]

Conant then built a small gymnasium onto the west wall of the Academy building in 1895 to provide a larger exercise area. The Academy adopted the Emersonian system of physical culture described as "psycho-physical training based on Physiological and Psychological laws." This was a system of physical culture and gymnastics that developed "not only health and strength, but also grace, beauty and the responsiveness of the body to mental attitude."[20] During the same period, the Nichols Academy Athletic Association was formed, although it did not become fully active until after 1900.[21]

In this transition era, student regulations also came under review – and old concerns came back into focus as noted in Principal Marcellus Coggan's regulations announced in 1878. Under a category of "Things Strictly Forbidden to All," he included improper language, smoking anywhere, and opening the boarding house doors at night. In a second or disciplinary category, "Marks of Deportment," the Academy began to total individual student's demerits (48 demerits ended one's stay at the Academy). These could be assigned for absences, disorderly or improper conduct in the boarding house (meeting guests away from the reception room, lateness for meals, failing to get permission to go into town, and not going to church on Sunday if on Dudley Hill). As for "Scholarship," students were ranked by monthly exams. Earning a grade of less than 50 percent on an exam meant the test had to be retaken. Monthly reports regarding both deportment and scholarship went to parents.[22] Many of these regulations had been in place for some time, but the fact that the process was being reemphasized and further systematized suggests a continuing need to communicate directly with parents and to hold students to stricter standards.

One fascinating aspect of a Nichols Academy education evolved around activities designed for the entire Academy. As in "old" Academy days, community learning remained a central part of the educational routine. Undoubtedly, this varied from one principal to the next, but careful descriptions in 1879 by Nichols Principal Edmund P. Barker, from Amherst and Deerfield Academy, and Preceptress Susan M. Barker, from Salem Normal School, provide a better picture of the post-1875 Nichols Academy program.

During the 1879 fall term, the Barkers skillfully fashioned a lively weekly program for the school community. Beginning with a daily reading from Shakespeare's "Merchant of Venice" by Mrs. Barker (pupils preparing for

Fig. 5.2. Topics, Nichols Academy Debating Society, 1880

NICHOLS ACADEMY DEBATING SOCIETY, 1880
Topics for Debate, Winter-Spring

"Resolved, that corporal punishment in schools should be abolished."
  Decided in the affirmative.

"Resolved, that the prosperity of this country demands General Grant for its next President."
  Decided a third term an "absurdity."

"Resolved, that the word "God" be inserted in the Constitution of the United States."
  Decided in the negative.

"Resolved, that cremation is a better way of disposing of bodies after death, than burial."
  Decided: the merit of the question was decided for the negative; the weight of the
  argument was won by the affirmative.

"Resolved, that a falsehood is sometimes justifiable."
  Decided in the negative.

"Resolved, that Caesar should command more praise for his military record than Napoleon."
  Decided for Napoleon.

"Resolved, that wealth is more powerful than education."
  Decided (unanimously) in the affirmative.

"Resolved, that the menta capacities of woman are not equal to those of men."
  Decided (unanimously) in the negative.

"Resolved, that the playing of baseball is an injury to the country."
  Decided: the merit of question for the negative, the weight of argument in affirmative.

"Resolved, that it would be for the best interests of all students to disband the Debating Society."
  Decided in the negative.

"Resolved, that lawyers are justified in defending Criminals."
  Decided in the negative.

"Resolved, the reading of Fiction is detrimental to Mankind."
  Decided in the negative.

Sources: *Webster Times*, January 7, 1880; Ibid., February 28, 1880; Ibid., March 6, 1880; Ibid., March 13, 1880; Ibid., April 17, 1880; Ibid., May 4, 1880, Ibid., May 22, 1880; Ibid., May 29; Ibid., June 12, 1880.

college were exempt), it also consisted of a daily spelling exercise for the whole school as well as daily gymnastics in the school hall for everyone. Rhetorical exercises were held weekly and free-hand drawing was offered to everyone, including townspeople. Under the Barkers, all Academy students had to write two impromptu compositions each term and one additional composition along with regular subject requirements. The Barkers also introduced brief, twice-daily singing sessions frequently accompanied by instrumental music. This gave everyone "much pleasure," according to their report.[23] A weekly debating society also became extremely active and successful. (See Fig. 5.2.) Beyond this, in warmer weather the Barkers frequently took the school on picnics to the "Narrows" at Webster Lake.[24]

With new, impressive buildings, a modernized "scientific" curriculum, and talented leadership, there is little question that Nichols trustees expected an increased enrollment. Unfortunately, this did not happen. Statistics gathered from meticulously prepared "Principal's Reports" between 1878 and 1901 show registration for separate terms consistently numbering between 30 and 50 students.[25] Total enrollment for the three terms in 1878–1879 was 151 students. Twenty years later, in 1901 and the last year of available principal's reports, the student enrollment was 141 for three terms or nearly the same as in 1879 suggesting that no substantial enrollment gains had been made. However, some institutional changes did occur. First, the number of young women in attendance started to increase again. The percentage of young ladies in each term climbed from 33 percent in 1884–1885 to 44 percent by the 1895–1896 academic year. It was up to 51 percent in 1901.[26] That year, their number surpassed the number of "Gentlemen" in each term. (See Appendix C.)

Second, prior to the Civil War, scholars at Nichols Academy in one year had come from as many as 32 communities in four states. This geographical distribution of students changed significantly after the Civil War due to the growth of new public high schools. Seventy-two percent of the 1880–1900 Nichols Academy's student population was composed of Dudley students technically attending Dudley High School at the Academy. (See Appendix D.) Twenty-eight percent of students at the Academy were formally enrolled in the preparatory school program. This was a telling change. The tendency to rely more and more on a local base, as solid as the numbers may have seemed, made the Academy more vulnerable to local conditions and attitudes. Then too, increases in the Dudley enrollment numbers held no financial benefits for the Academy since the town's fee for Dudley students was a flat $1,000, whether ten or one hundred town students enrolled.

While the relationship that evolved between the town and the Academy was successful, Dudley voters occasionally reviewed their options regarding "Dudley High School." In 1887, the Dudley Town Meeting considered a motion for discontinuing their "arrangement" with the Nichols Academy Board of Trustees and to "make provisions for creating a high school." It was passed over as soon as the question of financing was introduced.[27] How long the 1871 Dudley-Academy arrangement could continue was a logical question given the shifting pattern of cultural and population changes and underlying tensions within the community. Further, the unwillingness or inability of the town to build a new high school and the efforts of the Massachusetts Board of Education to control the nature of secondary education throughout the Commonwealth greatly complicated the issue.

As occurred in 1827, the 1871 agreement with the town required that the Academy formally establish admissions requirements. All Dudley candidates for admission to the Academy were examined in arithmetic, geography,

English grammar, reading, spelling and penmanship. Theoretically, acceptable preparation was based on a thorough knowledge of standard textbooks. In actuality, however, applicants had to successfully answer only three out of ten questions on a written admissions exam. Even the Dudley School Committee believed this was a very low standard.[28] Eventually these barely adequate requirements adversely affected the Academy's ability to educate Dudley students in four years.

Most Nichols Academy students did not pay any tuition during Mr. Conant's later years. This too was a dramatic change from the "old" Academy. By 1893–1894, no more than nine out of 169 scholars attending Nichols Academy were supported directly by their parents. Academy receipts from the year ending in June 1895 include funding from the Hancock Fund originally established in 1869 (interest on $6,000), the Congdon Fund (interest on $2,000), along with interest from a £32,000 fund established by Hezekiah Conant, $1,000 in accordance with the town of Dudley agreement, and $72 from the town of Charlton for its students at the Academy. Tuition paid by parents that year amounted to only $71.00 out of total Academy receipts of $4,293.95.[29] In 1900, only one tuition payment was made by a parent for an out-of-town student. The Hancock Fund that year supported 30 scholars, Dudley funds covered tuition for 73, Charlton paid for seven. However, by 1905, Charlton had constructed its own high school and its students no longer attended Nichols Academy.[30]

It was a pleasant experience to attend the Academy when one did not pay tuition of seven to ten dollars per term. However, this might not avoid additional costs. Room and board charges for boarding at Conant Hall were four to five dollars a week with students assured by the Academy that yearly boarding costs would not exceed $200. Interestingly, Academy catalogues also note that rooms in town could be obtained for 25 to 50 cents a week, perhaps costing as little as seventeen or eighteen dollars a year.[31] Nonetheless, even with tuition paid, not everyone could afford an Academy education. As for Nichols Academy, a look at the school in 1900 might have suggested that it was a wealthy institution without debts and with sufficient funds available for needy students. However, it could have been argued quite correctly that Nichols Academy did not have a large endowment compared with other small New England preparatory schools.

At the beginning of the twentieth century, the new Academy was markedly different from the Academy of fifty years before. Aside from completely new facilities built by Hezekiah Conant, the curriculum had been greatly influenced by Conant's interest in what he referred to as practical or applied science. Nonetheless, the Academy was still caught between those who wanted to use their secondary school education to prepare for life and those who saw college admission as the primary goal.

At Nichols Academy in 1900, eight graduated from the Literary and Scientific course, two from the Classical course, one from a Latin and Scientific course, and one from the Commercial course. The Academy focus on a college preparatory program or a Classical course had broadened somewhat, at least in the Academy's promotional literature. Graduates from the Literary and Scientific course were ready for entrance into "the best technical schools" such as MIT and WPI. This was a projected niche. The reality was that the Academy's student body in 1900 was smaller and much more geographically concentrated than in the past. It now primarily came from four south central Massachusetts communities (Dudley, Webster, Charlton, and Oxford) and several nearby Connecticut communities (Quinebaug, North Grosvenordale, and the Woodstocks) – all within a ten mile radius.[32] Conant had hoped to establish a scientific school, but this had not happened.

There were a number of other notable developments. The Academy continued to maintain that it was "free from the teaching of any sectarian principals of religion," while requiring its resident student body to attend church on Sundays. Some believed that an effort to establish religious associations for Academy students was beneficial due to the secular position being taken by public schools. Then too, daily student activities involved the library, observatory, boarding house, Academy building, and gymnasium. These buildings had not existed twenty-five years before. And, by November 1897, electric lights appeared on Dudley Hill although it would take time for them to reach into Academy buildings.[33]

THE CLASS OF '77

One of the more interesting and important developments at the Academy during this period was an increased desire to recognize the old school through various celebrations. When Hezekiah Conant joined the Nichols Academy board, he strongly supported and promoted activities that included the increasingly popular events surrounding the Academy's yearly graduations and the annual alumni reunions held in June. For instance, the celebration of the graduation of the Class of 1877 was meant to further promote traditions while recognizing the Academy's largest senior class in a number of years. In the process, school spirit increased enormously. A description of its graduation day is worth noting.

Activities opening the graduation celebration for the Class of '77 and the third annual alumni day actually began on Thursday, June 21, 1877. Public examinations and recitations for classes in geometry, algebra and arithmetic were held in the morning and Latin, Greek, botany, philosophy, grammar and reading in the afternoon. The next morning, with a bright sun overhead and a band on hand, the class tree was planted on the common and several poems and addresses were given. At nine o'clock, graduation exercises began in the Congregational Church. The eleven graduates read essays and then received diplomas from E. F. Smith, a member of the town school committee. Smith acknowledged that the promises of the Nichols trustees that led to the original contract between the town and the Academy in 1871 had been fully "realized." He felt that the town should be proud of its school.[34] The celebration, including a dinner and toasts in the Academy Hall, eventually ended that evening.

During the course of graduation day, a significant contribution to posterity was made by one of the members of the Class of '77 who presented the class statistics. This information was then included in an article on the graduation by a *Webster Times* reporter.[35] This report contained some of the vital statistics of class members as well as offering insights into their thinking, habits, and interests with a dash of tongue-in-cheek humor. Included in this information was the fact that every member of the class, nine young men and two women graduates, had received demerits at some point; one had even received a suspension. Also noted was the fact that two members had written poetry, another had tried and failed.

Clearly the Class of '77 was not large, either in number or in physical stature. According to the class statistics, as reported by the *Webster Times*, the oldest of the graduating class was 22 years of age while the youngest graduate was 17. The average age of the class was 18 years and six months while the average weight of the class was 137 pounds with the average height nearly five feet two inches. The tallest student was five feet eight inches, the shortest four feet seven inches.

As for their social relationships, as provided by the *Webster Times* reporter, the class statistician also presented some interesting details. For one, it was concluded that an engagement loomed for one of its members. Also asserted was that one of their class was "single out of principle" while the others were "unconditionally single." Another insight refers to two classmates who have had "just a little affection" for every assistant teacher who gave them instruction. And, in a final detail, the statistician concludes that one member of the class "never" flirts, but ten always do.[36]

Our inquiring statistician continued his survey "as regards the weed" and intoxicating beverages. It is disclosed that "four never smoke," but seven do. Of the smokers, one of this group is a hard smoker, one only smokes cigars, one just cigarettes, with four apparently ready to smoke anything. Three members of the class are only occasional smokers, one smokes "semi-occasionally," and three smoke all the time. Two also chew tobacco. As for intoxicating liquors, the class statistics show that nine of eleven apparently do not indulge. Five drink soda water, two pure H_2O, one sweetened water, one Baptist beer (probably alcohol-free beer), one drinks anything but water, and one never refuses anything. Our seemingly erstwhile statistician perceptively adds as an after thought that "some who drink say nothing about it."

Revealed too are significant examples of surprising diversity. Clearly the Academy's once rural society no longer could be seen as a solid block. Politics and religion are cases in point. Although only one of its number voted, the Class of '77 was divided almost equally between five members who seemed to be Democrats and four who preferred the Republican party. Two in the class were on the fence. This diversity is likewise reflected in the religious beliefs of the class where four were listed as Congregationalists, three were Roman Catholics, one was a Universalist, one an Episcopalian, one a free thinker, and one apparently undecided.

Not surprisingly, the Class of '77 also demonstrated a similar lack of agreement regarding future personal goals. According to the statistician's survey, as reported in the *Webster Times*, one classmate intended to go into medicine, and another into law. The rest were undecided although their interests went from a desire to be president of the United States to one who wanted to become an "organ grinder."[37]

Several interesting and important details remain regarding the members of the Class of '77 and their futures. All "gentlemen" graduates of Nichols Academy in 1877 were going to college. Five were going to Williams College, while one each was going to Dartmouth, Harvard, Amherst, and Bowdoin. No mention is made of the two young women. And, as a proper ending for the Academy's graduation day, the Academy "base ball nine" easily beat Putnam 9 to 0 that afternoon.[38]

Clearly this statistical study is incomplete since it did not distinguish between young men and young women leaving some unanswered questions. Nonetheless, the nature of the survey, the topics it covered, and some of the results say much about this society and the young people who were just leaving the Academy in 1877. Humor may have been a large part of this statistical presentation but the overall results are extremely helpful in understanding a group of Academy students. When these Class of '77 statistics and the topics selected by the Nichols Academy Debating Society three years later are placed side-by-side, high levels of maturity, sensitivity and achievement are demonstrated by this group of Nichols Academy graduates. (See Fig. 5.2.) Clearly they were very bright young people. Some, if not all, of the Class of 1877 may be present in the picture of the Nichols Academy campus and its students taken between 1874 and 1880. (See photograph of Nichols Academy, ca. 1878, on cover and on page 8.)

LIFE IN THE ACADEMY IN THE 1880s

As Nichols Academy entered the 1880s, it appeared positioned to achieve even greater recognition. Its new buildings – the Academy building and Hall, Conant Library and Observatory, and Roger Conant Hall (replacing the Boarding House in 1885) – offered a small and unparalleled campus. (See pictures on pages 8-9.) Although small, it gained a reputation as a staunch rural New England academy. The Academy's agreement in 1871 with the town of Dudley had it serving as Dudley High School thereby creating a critical enrollment base as well as firmly establishing a relationship between the town and the Academy. And, last but not least, Hezekiah Conant's enthusiastic support for both town and Academy seemed to predict a successful future.

In 1884, Nichols Academy registered a total of 144 students over three separate but consecutive terms in 1883-1884. This enrollment counted one person three times if he or she were present for three terms. That year the Academy's total enrollment was made up of 55 percent males and 45 percent females. Of the total enrollments, 60 percent came from Dudley; females made up 49 percent of the Dudley total. (See Appendix C.)

But what can be said about life in Mr. Conant's Academy? Fortunately several former Academy students have commented in detail about some of their activities at the Dudley Hill School. Charles L. Robinson '84, George J.

The Class of 1884 and their Instructors
Front row: Charles L. Robinson, George J. Searle, Frank Goodman, Jennie Bates and Charles Thompson. *Rear row*: Ann M. Alton, Principal Fred E. Corbin, and Assistant Principal Clara K. Goodwin. Source: *The Nichols Alumnus*, Vol. 1, June 1947, No. 3, 1.

The Boarding House (1873-1883)
Source: "Catalogue and Program," Nichols Academy,
Dudley, Massachusetts, 1878, cover.

Searle '84, and Channing M. Wells '86 attended the Academy between 1883 and 1886. They came from different backgrounds and provide important recollections of their experiences. When placed side-by-side, their stories offer a comprehensive and fascinating picture of life on the Hill in the 1880s.

Perhaps the best description of the Academy from the student's perspective comes from Charles L. Robinson, a Connecticut resident. His account of dormitory conditions in 1883, the year that the Boarding House burned to the ground, offers wonderful observations about life there. This three-story building, four in the back, built in 1873, was hardly comfortable during cold weather. It featured "generous drafts" through the cracks and openings. One such opening, according to Robinson, occurred when a back door was opened

NICHOLS ACADEMY: THE SPRING ON THE HILL ∽

for expeditions to a small rear building which housed what was referred to as "exterior plumbing," although no plumbing existed. The dormitory had no plumbing or central heating and got its water from a well which then flowed out through a sink drain in the kitchen.[39]

Student rooms, according to Robinson, were hardly "modern." They were furnished with a wooden bed and a feather mattress resting on crossed ropes. As he recalled, the student rooms had a "chest of drawers with a looking glass above, a pine table and chair, a pine wash stand that was box-like with a lid that contained the usual bedroom crockery – pitcher, bowl, a combination of drinking, shaving and tooth mug. . . . a tin slop jar on the side, completed the toilet arrangements."[40]

Heat, when it was available in the dormitory, came from iron stoves with wood boxes and a pan of shavings. Ice frequently was found in the water pitcher. Cord wood was available but it had to be split and cost 5 cents a bushel. Importantly, a spark from an open damper landed in a wood box in 1883 and the building burned to the ground.

Included in the three dollars a week board was their food. Described by Robinson, food at the old boarding house was "scanty." "Potatoes and vegetables were fillers, corn beef Thursday, fish Friday, baked beans Saturday, chicken – water-fowl anyway – Sundays."[41] Bread was baked once a week and brushed over with hot lard.

In 1883, Robinson described members of the student body as falling into three categories. The "boarding scholars," referred to by Robinson as "nabobs," the day scholars who lived within walking distance and who always had impressive lunches, and those who found accommodations in rooms over Dudley Hill sheds at 50 cents a week.[42]

The shed dwellers came with "a five-day supply of bread, baked beans and doughnuts that could be supplemented at the store on Dudley Hill with Boston crackers, cheese, smoked herring, and fair-sized popcorn balls, which like the dried herring, were 1 cent per."[43] Robinson clearly enjoyed his time in "student nests" usually heated by an old cook stove to about 110 degrees and featured rough-housing usually followed by occasional fights. He described it a "wonderful atmosphere for arguments on school politics, games of old sledge with worn out cards, during the confusion a few boys busily worked on their problems in math and geometry."[44]

Robinson praised their attitudes. "It was in their shed rooms that students, handicapped by lack of money, were forced to struggle for the education that their ambition and courage demanded for them. Lack of decent clothes and even hunger could not stop them."[45]

One such fellow was George J. Searle, Robinson's friend and classmate. Searle was born and received his early education in London. However, his life

Channing M. Wells '86
Channing Wells '86, taken while president of the
American Optical Company about 1938.
Source: "Nichols Academy in 1886," *The Nichols Alumnus*,
Vol. 2, June 1948, No. 3, 3.

in Rhode Island had been difficult and he had been working as a laborer in the
Conant mill in Pawtucket when he decided to attend Nichols Academy. At 21
he began at the Dudley academy. He managed to get a room in a deserted
house that cost him $44 a term even though it was so cold that his ink froze in
its bottle at night. Searle was employed at the Academy in his senior year as a
janitor at $2.50 a week. He cleaned out classrooms, the Assembly Hall, lit
stoves, kept the library fire going, read meteorological instruments daily at 9
p.m. (readings went to Washington, D.C. once a week), and shoveled snow off
walks in wintertime.[46]

Dr. Searle had once said at Nichols that he "always wanted to practice
medicine and knew that he should know something about anatomy.
Consequently, with Charles Robinson, his friend and classmate, he visited
Burnet's [Burnett's] Farm evenings to catch rats in the dairy barn [now Daniels
Auditorium on the Nichols College campus] to use for experimentation."[47] The
day after graduating from Nichols Academy, Searle walked from Dudley to
Boston. He then graduated with a medical degree from Boston University
Medical School in 1888.

Soon after Charles L. Robinson and George Searle left Nichols Academy,
Channing M. Wells '86 from nearby Southbridge enrolled at the Dudley
School. His Academy experience and background differed somewhat from
Robinson and Searle. His account of his Nichols days offers yet another side of
life at Nichols Academy.

Channing Wells, it appears, was one of the students that Robinson referred to as "boarding scholars." His account of life at Nichols Academy focused on his time in the new dormitory built in 1885 by Hezekiah Conant which he named Roger Conant Hall (later referred to as the Dudley Inn). He said that it had "excellent rooms" and that each student took care of his or her rooms.[48] Wells recalled how proud he was in his first year at the Academy. He felt he had a fine corner room.[49] He also commented that they had their meals in the dormitory, probably in the basement, where the students and four teachers sat at a very long table. They had "good times" at their table.[50]

Important for Channing Wells were his principal and teachers who he described with great sensitivity. Mr. Emerson Clark was the principal. A former head of a military academy, Wells felt he ran Nichols Academy "on somewhat of the same basis." He was "perhaps on the severe side but not too much so."[51] Wells noted too that the faculty included a Miss Rose of Worcester and Mr. Rollin Tyler of Connecticut and a graduate of Yale. They were, for Wells, two of the better teachers in his entire educational experience.

Baseball was one of Wells' interests. It was the only organized sport on the campus in 1885 although an exercise gymnasium existed in the basement of the Academy building at that time. Wells was captain of the Nichols Academy baseball team coached by instructor Rollin Tyler, a former Yale athlete, who was interested in organizing a baseball team. Wells believes he was team captain because his father had a horse and carryall that could carry many ball players to games. Nichols primary opponent this year was Woodstock Academy, just a few miles into Connecticut.[52]

The Academy's baseball captain recalled that the Conant family visited the Academy dormitory on occasion. Hezekiah Conant then offered Academy students friendly and helpful advice. His son, Samuel M. Conant, occasionally stayed in the new dormitory clearly impressing the students. His highly polished English boots were looked at with awe by Wells' fellow students. Samuel Conant also had a mustache with ends twisted into sharp points.

Like George Searle had done, Channing Wells also worked in the Library and Observatory keeping records and making out weather reports. In his case he received $5 a sesson and "enjoyed it very much."[53]

Wells also discussed his transportation to and from Nichols Academy. Each week he took the 7 o'clock train from Southbridge to Quinebaug and walked up the hill to the Academy, a two-mile walk that he described as "delightful."[54] And occasionally he would cheerfully share his access to a horse and sleigh with his girl friends who attended Nichols from Southbridge.

Sometimes others took advantage of railroad transportation. In the early days, the Academy had to be reached by foot, stage coach, horseback or horse-drawn carriage. By 1840 and the construction of the Norwich & Worcester

Railroad depot in Webster, it was possible to take a train to Webster, three miles east of Nichols Academy and then walk or get a carriage to Dudley Hill.

Using the train was a logical approach but it was hardly simple. For instance, Clarence H. Knight, a student from Charlton, northwest of Dudley, described his weekly trip to the Dudley academy in 1898 and 1899 as "quite a journey."[55] On Monday mornings he took the early train from Charlton Depot to Worcester in central Worcester County, changed trains for Webster, and then walked the three miles to the Academy from Webster. He retraced his steps on Friday afternoons. This was just part of the price Knight had to pay to attend the Academy. Eventually this was to be a simple nine-mile trip by automobile.

Channing Wells wrote at the end of his message how "fortunate he was to attend Nichols at that time." He also said he experienced "the most pleasant recollections of my life there and realize that I accomplished and learned more there than I had been able to in the public schools."[56]

THE LEGACY OF HEZEKIAH CONANT

Hezekiah Conant died at his home in Pawtucket, Rhode Island, on January 22, 1902, at the age of seventy-five. At the time of his death, commentators spoke glowingly about the man and his contributions. According to one:

> He brought to his life's work an unusual sense of intelligence, especially in all mechanical matters, and by thrift, painstaking industry, energy and perseverance . . . . [he was] simple and democratic in his habits, he allowed no material prosperity to destroy those early tastes which made him love the common people. [He was] . . . a man of unimpeachable integrity, honest in speech and deed. . . .[57]

Another added that Conant "had a magnetic personality, great personal charm and simple and democratic habits, with a keen intellect, and a genius for organization."[58] Standing just over five-feet, one-half inch in height, and weighing only 125 pounds, Conant also was an inventor of note.[59] He was a true representative of the late nineteenth century American industrial society in every respect. His son, Samuel Morris Conant, later described him as an "old-fashioned type of gentleman," who resembled "Benjamin Franklin with a dash of Abraham Lincoln humor."[60]

Townspeople believed that he had saved Amasa Nichols' school from closing. The *Academy Bell*, a publication intended to provide information for the Dudley Hill community from the Academy, the First Congregational Church, and the Village Improvement Society, called him the "Second Founder" of the Academy. The *Bell* concluded "that Nichols Academy would have terminated its work years before but for the timely assistance of Hezekiah

Conant."[61] Reverend Goodell referred to him as an "intimate friend" who headed the most successful manufacturing enterprise in Rhode Island.[62] Most believed that under Conant's leadership, Nichols Academy became a viable institution, one that established a base for a twentieth century college.

More specifically, he had reconstructed the Academy campus by building a level plateau on the top of Dudley Hill in the late 1870s. Between 1881 and 1885, he constructed three major buildings for his former school: the Academy building, Conant Library and Observatory, and a boarding house named Roger Conant Hall. Ten years later he added a gymnasium to the west side of the Academy building. He then constructed two other secondary buildings – a barn or carriage house to the rear of Conant Hall and a small wooden transit house next to his Library and Observatory. Despite years of change, Conant's buildings still serve as examples of 19th century architecture and campus development and have become landmarks on the Dudley Hill skyline. Indeed, the institution had become Mr. Conant's academy. And, for most of this period, he had actually owned a large part of it.

While his contribution to the Nichols campus is easily identified, it is not as simple to assess Conant's leadership as president of the Academy's board of trustees. Not surprisingly, his professional success and enthusiasm for the Academy influenced its direction and course offerings. This was important for him. His internationally recognized abilities in clock making were related to his great interest in meteorology which led to a telegraphy program and the creation of a volunteer U.S. Signal Corps station in his Library and Observatory building. The Academy curriculum in 1900 included a strong scientific leaning that he aggressively promoted. While Conant was not an educator, and he did not claim to be one, he was charting the Academy's direction.

Conant's effort to "resuscitate" the Academy and Dudley Hill went far beyond the actual Academy campus. When the First Congregational Church at the top of Dudley Hill burned to the ground in 1890, he again had the opportunity to assist his former home town. Immediately he offered to replace this structure. His new building, now the First Congregational Church of Dudley, United Church of Christ, Conant Memorial, was built in classic Romanesque style and easily became the largest and most impressive structure in Dudley. The bell tower of the Conant Memorial Church featured four large dials and a clock which Conant designed with unique interacting pendulums and other improvements of his making.[63] This church remains an architectural masterpiece.

His intention was to memorialize his ancestors while putting "in the hands of the people of Dudley a useful structure, a convenient place of worship, and a house where they can sit sheltered from chilling winds or falling rain or scorching sun. . . . "[64] When he rebuilt the First Congregational Church in 1891, he expected Academy students to attend services there and to hold their "annual exercises at the close of the academic year" in this building as they had done before.[65]

Probably at Conant's urging, the town of Dudley decided to build a new grammar school between the new Congregational Church and the Academy's Conant Hall.[66] To make sure that the new grammar school reflected the architecture of the surrounding Conant-financed structures, Charles F. Wilcox, a long-recognized church architect from Providence, Rhode Island, and the architect for the Conant Memorial Church, helped to design the town's new Center School completed in 1893.[67] These structures had come from Conant's desires to improve the old Academy, to recognize the Conant family, and to re-energize Dudley Hill. Three of the five buildings on Dudley Hill bear the Conant name. How well he did his work is evidenced by the fact that four of these five buildings remain virtually intact while the fifth (the Academy building) is still in place despite experiencing significant damage during the hurricane of 1938. The Conant Memorial Church remains his most significant single achievement.

Conant's role in community development went beyond the Academy buildings and the First Congregational Church. By 1880, he had begun to acquire and build additional property on Dudley Hill.[68] His summer residence, Budleigh Hall, constructed in 1888 to the south of the Academy buildings, was named for his ancestral home in the parish of East Budleigh in Devonshire, England.[69] The size and beauty of this building virtually dominated a hill top he now partially owned. At the time of his death, his summer estate in Dudley included one main house, five other houses, four barns, one cider mill, store houses, one clubhouse, one windmill, one water tank, four horses, and eight cows. The area for his summer home and adjacent property easily exceeded 100 acres by 1900.[70]

In a period of about twenty years, Hezekiah Conant had preserved an educational center, reactivated Dudley Hill as a social center, rebuilt a religious center, constructed a family memorial on Dudley Hill, and built a widely admired summer estate. His specific contributions changed the contour and context of the center of Dudley, introduced buildings of architectural importance, and imposed a distinct design that would be difficult to alter. The grand result of Conant's financing was a new skyline for Dudley Hill formed by nineteenth century architecture that bestowed a permanent commitment and crown of beauty on the hill top. Beyond this, he reestablished the village of Dudley Hill at a time when it appeared incapable of retaining a prominent position in the town of Dudley. He reset the standard for the Hill. His efforts reintroduced elements of aesthetics and nineteenth century spiritual values that featured lifelong learning, family, a commitment to Christian life, a sense of home, beauty, and style. And, by example, he conveyed the message that stewardship was crucial if a society was to benefit from its prosperity. As for the Academy, Conant simply stated that "she is my western college. . . ."[71]

Aside from rejuvenating both the Academy and the village of Dudley Hill, Hezekiah Conant also worked to bring them closer together. His buildings – the Conant Library and Observatory, the Academy building, and Roger Conant Hall (called the Dudley Inn) – were available for use by both Academy students and townspeople. When Conant became an Academy trustee, the Board of Trustees was in the process of organizing "a reunion of graduates, teachers, patrons and friends of the institution."[72] Not only did he enthusiastically support these celebrations, he eventually became president of the Academy Alumni Association and personally brought large numbers of Rhode Islanders to yearly June alumni celebrations that coincided with Academy graduations. These were gala occasions for old Dudley Hill with its visitors arriving in Webster on the train and then taken to the Academy in horse-drawn carriages.

The *Academy Bell* also emphasized that the strength of the institution was embedded in its earlier years noting that "few of the New England academies have had such a strong local constituency and such sturdy support from their own towns as had been enjoyed by this institution since its incorporation in 1819."[73] This was a tribute to Amasa Nichols, the Academy trustees, Dudley town leaders, Dudley voters, Hezekiah Conant, and a number of preceptors and principals. The *Academy Bell* was right. A reporter's brief newspaper article twenty years later appropriately and perceptively observed that "it is the grouping of these circumstances that has made Dudley Hill one of the most unique little villages in New England."[74]

CHAPTER 6

THE SEARCH FOR A LARGER FIELD OF USEFULNESS

Nichols Academy's role as a direct provider of secondary education ended when it stopped enrolling students in 1909. This closing should not have been surprising. Only 11 percent of America's secondary school students then were in private schools.[1] However, this was not the end of Nichols Academy or its influence. Its buildings made up one of the finer, small academy campuses in rural Massachusetts. Further, the long-existing spirit and purpose of the institution were not forgotten and became even greater influences on Academy trustees. Reverend Charles L. Goodell, then president of the Academy Board of Trustees, noted in 1923 that the trustees believed that the "fine buildings, erected and equipped . . . by Mr. Hezekiah Conant, ought to be utilized for a work in harmony with the purpose of its founder to help deserving young people to a better education."[2] The trustees' task after 1909 was to find an acceptable tenant for their campus. Between 1909 and 1931, three potential occupants appeared: the Dudley school system; the Bethel Bible Institute from Spencer, Massachusetts; and a junior college of business administration program operating in New Hampshire.

THE EDUCATIONAL EFFORTS OF THE ACADEMY AND THE TOWN

Nichols Academy seemed positioned to move easily into the next century despite the passing of Hezekiah Conant in 1902. Historically, the ability and willingness of town leaders to support the institution and the educational needs of its students led to close ties with the Academy. With time, these connections seemed to be growing stronger as Nichols Academy served as both Dudley's High School and as a preparatory or "fitting" school for the best eastern colleges. Then too, the involvement of local Academy graduates as teachers in Dudley elementary schools made the relationship even closer. Progress, however, now depended on the ability to change, rather than on a continued reliance on past accomplishments.

Over time, more and more public high schools and parochial schools emerged throughout the area providing education at little direct cost to these students. This meant fewer students for private academies. And, where curriculum development had once been a primary concern and strength of local academies, by 1900 most decisions regarding curriculum matters and directions for secondary schools were made by the Massachusetts Department of Education or by college admissions departments. Between 1902 and 1909, the tensions created by these forces pulled at the foundation of Nichols Academy. It was too much. Nichols Academy simply ran out of students by 1909. When the Academy closed, one reporter wrote: "the old academy, once one of the leaders of Worcester county preparatory schools, and with a career dating back to 1819, is about to give up the ghost."[3] He was right – to a point.

Enrollment at the Dudley academy had begun to slide even before Conant's death in 1902. An aggregate of 141 students registered over three terms in 1901 with an average attendance of 47 scholars per term. Thirty-six out of the 54 students who enrolled that year came from Dudley with four from Charlton. There generally were more women than men in the Academy student body. In June 1901, Principal Alfred Collins and his two assistants graduated five students. Not one parent paid tuition charges, although the tax payers of Dudley and Charlton were responsible for their students.[4]

To meet the challenge of a new century, a number of important additions were made to restructure the Academy's appeal and to make it "rank with the best preparatory schools for colleges and scientific institutions in the country."[5] This upgrading included refocusing the curriculum and adding to extracurricular offerings. Although the Academy experienced curriculum expansion during the Conant era, a consistent and expansive approach was not possible to maintain when enrollment numbers began to fall.

Formal athletics and extracurricular activities were added to the Academy's offerings. This was consistent with the practices of other New England preparatory schools seeking to expand student activities. Academy publications after 1896 always mention the Academy's gymnasium, more of a large exercise room than a basketball court, which was used for physical exercise and basketball practice, if not games. Former Nichols Academy student, Clarence H. Knight, a member of the Academy basketball team in 1898 and 1899, recalled playing some games by the light of kerosine lanterns hung in the Academy Hall.[6]

Organized athletics were sponsored by the Nichols Academy Athletic Association, which supported teams in football, basketball and baseball. Reorganization of the football team was discussed in 1904 by the *Academy Bell*, which reported that "the school has been without one [a football team] for several years."[7] This is not the case with basketball as the Academy played a number of its basketball games in the Academy Hall against local high schools. Given declining enrollment numbers, it is remarkable that they were able to support any athletic teams at all.

Nichols Academy also made an effort to increase student involvement in religious activities to offset the secular attitudes of public high schools. This was not an unusual move by a New England preparatory school in 1900. The Dudley academy required that students on Dudley Hill attend the Conant Memorial Church on Sunday and made its minister an ex-officio member of the Academy Board of Trustees. Nichols Academy students also were invited to attend the Congregational Church's Bible School, while "devotional" exercises for the entire school were conducted each day. The goal of the Academy was "to cultivate a natural and healthy religious life in those committed to its care."[8] But this emphasis had to be applied selectively since students of "the High School at Nichols Academy" could not be required to participate.

Adjustments and decisions regarding the institution's direction were being made virtually all the time, but could proceed only so far. In a report to Dudley's superintendent of schools in 1904, Academy Principal Franklin C. Johnson discussed the success they were having with courses in practical agriculture such as animal husbandry, the study of fertilizers and crops, and dairy farming. He reported these subjects had evoked "considerable interest" from pupils and their parents, and he hoped that the Nichols trustees would continue to support them.[9] The *Academy Bell* agreed with Principal Johnson regarding the benefit of agricultural courses, as did most of the Dudley Hill population, but nothing further was done. Apparently, this was a belated stand for practical education being taken by a rural community. In an Academy announcement for 1904–1905, Johnson seemed to end the discussion by pointing out that the Academy now was offering two clearly defined courses: the Classical and the Literary and Scientific.[10] Both were college preparatory in nature. The "dual" nature of the Academy's program had ended. The Commercial course, as it had existed, no longer was available for Academy students.

Principal Johnson had walked into an educational storm. Although there had been a desire on the part of previous generations to support a dual program – one for college and one for practical and useful training – probably no one could have avoided the battle about to be fought. On the national level, a "Report of the Committee on Secondary School Studies in 1893" (sometimes referred to as the "Report of the Committee of Ten") concluded that there was no difference between academic and practical programs. The Committee of Ten determined that "Life and college were best prepared for by a mental discipline through the study of academic subjects."[11] This topic had been discussed by the Nichols Academy Board of Trustees many times since Principal Marcellus Coggan had introduced the issue of "fitting for college" in the 1870s. In effect, the Academy had been "fitting" its students for college while honoring its agreement with the town of Dudley to educate students who had practical needs. This had been its way since 1819.

Samuel W. Hallett replaced Johnson as Nichols Academy Principal in September 1905 introducing yet another era in the Academy's history. Regrettably, it was the last. Hallett's yearly reports to the Dudley school superintendent over the next three years spelled out new directions being taken by the Academy. For one, the Nichols trustees determined that tuition required from pupils outside Dudley had to be increased significantly although some income was being received from the Hancock, Congdon, and Conant Trusts.

Second, all subordinate subjects, such as those in agriculture recently discussed by Principal Johnson, were eliminated. The Academy was now guided, according to Hallett, by one goal: "to take its place among the educational institutions of the country as a college preparatory school."[12] In effect, the Academy was rejecting its historic role of providing both a classical and a practical education for interested Nichols Academy students. Hallett and most Nichols trustees accepted the philosophy of Harvard University President Charles W. Elliott, quoted by Hallett as saying that "Fitting for college is the same as fitting for life." This had been the conclusion of the report from the "Committee of Ten."

Subjects had to be taught the same way for everyone; all subjects had to have equal educational value. Everyone had to take the same subjects. According to this thinking, "a truly democratic school system" would then emerge. Such an educational process theoretically provided subjects rich in content and promised to be more contributive to the intellects of students during a critical time of their lives. Principal Hallett believed that "Nichols Academy, if it is to be a success, must stand for some well defined purpose." There can be no question that the Academy trustees were probably divided on this issue, but they eventually approved the position announced by the Academy's principal.[13]

According to Hallett, the school now "offers a course of study leading primarily to our best colleges, scientific schools, and state normal schools. It concentrates its resources to this purpose." He recognized that this did not please everyone, but he believed that student preparation "for the best colleges is almost fundamental to our generation." To support the success of the Nichols "fitting" school approach, Hallett identified recent Academy graduates then attending Harvard, WPI, MIT, Bowdoin, Norwich, and Princeton.[14]

Interestingly, and almost unnoticed in the process of rededicating the Academy was the fact it was available only for boys. In 1907–1908, the school Catalogue referred to Dudley Hill as "an ideal spot for a boys' school."[15] Earlier catalogues had fully documented the presence of women at Nichols Academy. Paradoxically, this decision regarding "boys' school" status could not be applied directly to students of Dudley High School at Nichols Academy; many were young women. In effect, two schools were existing in one.

Hallett's successor as Academy principal in 1908, Ernest T. Chase, eventually was able to provide the best assessment of the situation. Since he was new to the Academy, Chase reviewed previous communications with the town of Dudley and sought to address issues that he saw evolving because the Academy also acted as Dudley High School. His letter to Dudley School Superintendent Robinson that year was direct and thorough. He recognized the "dual nature" of the Academy and the reality of the need for two separate courses: one to prepare students for institutions of higher education and the other suited for students who were going out to work immediately after the Academy. He felt that one course should not negatively affect the other. But, according to Chase, the Commonwealth of Massachusetts required that all secondary school pupils be fit for state normal schools, technical schools, and colleges. He promised that he would try to pay attention to the needs of all students, but concluded there was little further he could do.[16]

Dudley Superintendent Robinson then commented on the Academy's situation and Chase's position in his "Annual Report" to the town. Robinson, also an Academy trustee, observed that "Each year seems to increase the difficulty [of the Academy] in filling the dual function of public and private school." This was, in his opinion, "a difficulty which many other similar institutions have had to meet and adjust definitely and permanently."[17] Clearly this was the challenge to the Academy.

Serious institutional deficiencies existed and the Academy trustees understood this. Robinson was right. For one, there were too few students at Nichols Academy to permit the development of satisfactory dual programs. In 1908–1909, there were 20 Dudley students in the Academy with one other student from out-of-town. Second, and not to be overlooked, according to Principal Chase, Dudley students at the Academy were poorly prepared for the high school work now being required since many came from Dudley's one-room district schools with eight grades. Chase stated that Webster High School required that such students take a preparatory or sub-freshman year before beginning four years in high school studies. Apparently, the Academy could have only four years with its Dudley students, probably due to its initial agreement with the town.

Chase argued that the town of Dudley "should not expect Nichols Academy to do work which ought to be done by the [town's elementary] schools." He felt that the Academy's task was being "severely handicapped." The solution was to make sure that students were better prepared before entering the Academy; he believed this was the responsibility of Dudley's school system.[18] Since the Academy closed the following June, this point was never addressed again.

Academy leadership appears to have been lacking at this point, as well, although a full assessment of the trustees' actions is not possible.[19] After Conant's death, his son, Samuel Morris Conant, took over as president of the board of trustees. But even after the Academy made a commitment to college preparatory programs, the school did not appear to accept this as the primary institutional objective until 1907.[20] Its 1871 agreement with the town clearly delayed the Academy's transition to a complete college preparatory program. Yet the Academy trustees were committed to their local students. Moreover, Hezekiah Conant had introduced many new ideas that reflected his somewhat narrow interests to promote and improve the Academy. It was possible that he was too attached to the past, to his home town and old school, to realize that change was producing a more complex and dynamic society.

Although enrollment details for its last few hours are not as available as in previous years (in itself a sign of institutional difficulties), declining numbers point to trying times. Finally, on Friday, June 18, 1909, Nichols Academy and Dudley High School graduated its last three students: two young Dudley women, Ethel Hiscox and Marion J. Durfee, and Leroy L. Taft from Union, New Hampshire. At that point, there were only eight students at the school, seven from Dudley.[21] The difficult decision to close the Academy was made by the trustees despite aggressive efforts taken after 1901 to improve the enrollment. But projections of only eight students for 1909–1910 did not support its continuation (For enrollment figures for Nichols Academy, see Appendix C.)

THE END OF A NOBLE EXPERIMENT ~ 1909

Academy trustees Conant, Jillson, Thayer, and the Reverend Dr. Charles L. Goodell had been fully committed to their old school; but there was no one like Monroe Nichols to lead it into the twentieth century. Men such as Alfred G. Collins, principal from 1889–1902 and a friend of Hezekiah Conant, and Earnest T. Chase, principal in 1908, understood the problem. So did Principal Franklin C. Johnson. This was a perplexing time. Becoming an expensive boarding school might have been one solution. To have done this, however, the Academy had to reject its beginnings that involved a nearly century-long commitment to the educational needs of a rural society and for a dual curriculum.

Perhaps not surprisingly, Nichols Academy trustees and principals were not alone in dealing with the difficulties of an academy-town partnership. This was a product of their times. Nearby Woodstock Academy, across the valley in Connecticut, was experiencing some of the same issues that confronted Nichols Academy after 1900. Discussions occurring in Woodstock also focused on Woodstock Academy's relationship with the town, the question of agricultural subjects, the meaning of a long historical connection with the townspeople, and the "economic restraint of the town." Woodstock resolved these issue differently than did Dudley. In 1913, the Woodstock voters determined that Woodstock Academy was to be the public high school of the town of Woodstock.[22] Then too, once flourishing Leicester Academy in central Massachusetts also experienced difficult times. After being closed several years, it combined with the town high school from 1867 until 1917, when the town was prohibited by the state from using public funds for a private school. It then discontinued operations.[23] Nichols Academy had been confronted by essentially the same challenging circumstances.

Nichols Academy closed its doors in 1909 because there were too few students. Clearly, this was a reason for closing; but it does not explain why there were insufficient numbers. For one, the Academy's role as a leader of locally-based secondary education had been taken over by the Massachusetts Board of Education and local public school systems. When a college-aimed educational program emerged as the central force in secondary school education, it was too late for a rural-based Massachusetts academy to respond. Clearly the "fitting for college – fitting for life" approach did not appeal to the Nichols Academy community.

Moreover, and perhaps most importantly, the Nichols Academy trustees apparently had not paid attention to the shift of the local population center from Dudley Hill to the French River area, now a potentially destructive force opposed to locating a high school on Dudley Hill. And, finally, it failed because those close to the Academy held its past in such high regard they did not recognize that the Academy had to satisfy present and future educational needs and realities. Paying homage to past achievements was not sufficient.

In a final statement, Ernest Robinson, the Dudley (and Webster) school superintendent, who also was a trustee of Nichols Academy, paid a brief but meaningful tribute to the Academy in his 1910 "Report to the Dudley School Committee." First, he recognized Nichols Academy for its "highly honorable and valuable educational service for Dudley and for Massachusetts." He also hoped ". . . that the present cessation of operations may be only temporary, as a preparation for another long-term period of educational uplift to the town and state."[24] But the Academy had stopped admitting students and a remarkable era had ended. For nearly a century, Nichols Academy made education a vital dimension of one small part of rural America. In Reverend Goodell's words, it was "second only to the Church." The Academy made it possible for a large group of rural Americans to meet the challenges and savor the potential of a remarkable century at relatively little cost. These men and women then helped to transform America – and Dudley.

A SCHOOL FOR THE TOWN?

When the Nichols Academy Board of Trustees announced in 1909 that the Academy was not going to reopen the next September, it immediately offered the town of Dudley the use of the Academy building for the following year.[25] Apparently there were no plans beyond that.[26] The town, however, hesitated. The realization that significant funds had to be used to maintain the Academy building as a public high school had not occurred to many. Making the decision difficult for the Dudley School Committee and the voters was the fact that, although the School Committee had accepted the Trustee offer, only eight or nine Dudley students were at Nichols Academy the next year attending the "High School at Dudley Hill," as they called it, while 30 other Dudley students were going to Webster (later Bartlett) High School. The reason for this is clear. Approximately 50 percent of Dudley's secondary school population now lived in Dudley's industrial villages along the French River that separated Dudley and Webster. The high school of Dudley was at Nichols Academy in the historic and geographic center of town – over two miles away.[27]

Dudley's school committee decided that the town's voters had three choices. First, the High School at Dudley Hill could be maintained by the town and tuition paid for those students as well as for another group that attended high school in Webster. This was the status quo. Second, the town could choose to have the school on Dudley Hill established as the town high school and connections with Webster discontinued. Third, they could erect a high school in the part of town where a majority of the children lived – near Webster and the French River. The school committee then concluded that the issue could not be resolved to "satisfy all the people in the town" and little progress was made.[28] The town proceeded to use the Nichols Academy building for lower-level high school students from the Dudley Hill area while also paying the tuition of Dudley students going to Webster and, in several cases, to Southbridge to the west.

While 30 Dudley pupils went to Webster High School in 1910, the town of Dudley continued to discuss possible arrangements with the Nichols Academy trustees. In the process, town officials determined that state law required the town to make significant improvements in the ventilation, heating, and sanitation systems of the nearly forty-year-old Academy building. The town believed that these costs should be divided between the town and the Academy; the Academy trustees disagreed.[29] Further, there was a question regarding the legality of using public money on private property. Little progress was made in these discussions, especially after a Dudley town meeting in 1916, when voters agreed to pay $63 per year for each Dudley pupil attending Bartlett (formerly Webster) High School. This vote highlighted Webster's willingness and ability to continue educating Dudley students and also confirmed that Dudley voters wanted it this way.[30]

Working relationships between the town and the Academy trustees achieved some stability as the town continued to use the Academy building for a lower-level high school.[31] Dudley school officials concluded that senior high school courses were more economical when taken at Bartlett High School. During the 1914–1915 school year, 23 students attended the High School at Dudley Hill, 42 went to Webster, and two enrolled at Southbridge High School. Still of concern was the Dudley elementary school system with eight, one-room schools, each serving eight grades, and three primary and grammar schools. This system produced students with varying skill levels, a condition that had to be corrected by taking an additional, or sub-freshman, year when they entered high school. Nichols Academy Principal Ernest Chase had noted this in 1908.

Academy trustees did not ignore the town's situation. Aside from allowing the town to use the Academy building, the Academy trustees voted in 1915 to give the town $700 a year to assist in maintaining "a four years high school."[32] They later revised their gift designation to apply to either junior or senior high school courses.[33] Furthermore, their interest in local education did not end there. In 1917, the Academy board attached a condition to their yearly gift declaring that it was to be used for "a course of domestic science or Household Arts" to be established at Dudley Hill.[34]

Essentially, a number of factors contributed to the inability of the Dudley school system to utilize the Nichols Academy building. Distance and related transportation costs, a perceived educational inferiority (Bartlett High School was a new and impressive building), general inconvenience, and continued town financial deliberations all worked against using the Dudley Hill location as a high school. Many Dudley citizens did not believe that the town could maintain a good school on Dudley Hill. The larger and newer high school in Webster seemed better. Others considered that the cost of transporting all students to Dudley Hill was too high. For instance, of the 41 Dudley students attending Bartlett (Webster) High School in 1922, 35 walked to classes in Webster over French River bridges. That year, aside from the 41 Dudley students at Bartlett High School, 15 were at Southbridge High School, two went to Worcester, and 22 were at the "High School at Dudley Hill."[35]

The lack of municipal direction also contributed to the difficulty of establishing a high school program on Dudley Hill. Between 1916 and 1923, the Dudley school committee and its school superintendent were considering the formation of a school union with Webster and even informally discussed a consolidation of the two towns. One strong recommendation included the building of a junior high school in the eastern part of the town closer to Webster and sending senior high school students to Bartlett High School.[36] Eventually a school union was formed, but discussions had been delayed too long to include the Dudley Hill location.

Also playing a role in this process was the Commonwealth of Massachusetts. State regulations spelled out the subjects to be taught and required that all students be introduced to the same course content. This was pointed out by the principal of Nichols Academy. He had preferred to tailor courses and subjects to individual needs, but state requirements dictated otherwise.[37] Then too, the state decreed in 1898 that "Every child between seven and 14 years of age shall attend some public school" where they reside.[38] The previous requirement had only been applied to children up to 12 years of age. One fundamental purpose of this law was to keep youths under 14 away from mill work.

As a result, however, a greater number of young men and women now were required to attend the lower high school grades thereby expanding the total number of older students in the Dudley school system and in the lower level high school. Many then left school at the age of 14. And, finally, whenever the town fathers discussed taking over the Nichols Academy building, they faced increased expenditures due to state structural requirements and costs for additional staffing. There can be no question that the town's long-standing fiscal conservatism greatly affected its eventual decision.[39]

There were other tasks for the Nichols Academy trustees apart from important discussions with Dudley school officials. While supporting annual gifts of $700 to the Dudley school system, they watched over the Dudley Inn (Conant Hall) and operated the Conant Library. Occasionally, the Academy trustees argued with the town regarding taxes on the Inn and threatened to deduct these taxes from the Academy's annual gift.

One important development occurred in 1921 when Reverend Charles L. Goodell became president of the Nichols Academy Board of Trustees. He had been a member of the trustees since 1876 and now was a nationally known Methodist minister and author who was about to introduce a significant radio program for NBC called "Sabbath Reveries." And, although local school issues and care for the Conant buildings were important and somewhat time consuming, the Academy board continued to look for opportunities to further utilize its property.[40]

Rev. Charles LeRoy Goodell, D.D. (1854–1937)
Member and president of Nichols Academy Board of Trustees, 1876–1929
Clergyman, "Shepherd of the Air," author of *Black Tavern Tales* and
numerous other books. Source: Charles Goodell, D.D., *Soul Reveries*
(New York: Fleming H. Revell Company, 1931) frontispiece.

"DUDLEY BIBLE INSTITUTE AND NICHOLS ACADEMY"

The last junior high school class graduated four young women and one young
man from the "High School at Dudley Hill" in June 1923. The Academy board
of trustees, not the Dudley school board, was responsible for the timing. That
year the Academy trustees had the opportunity to lease their buildings to the
Bethel Bible Institute of Spencer, Massachusetts.[41] Although the Dudley school
system had been using the Academy building less and less, the possibility that
it could be used by others apparently had not been anticipated by town
officials. Nonetheless, when Nichols Academy trustees had the chance, they
leased the hill top property.

Initial overtures from the Spencer-based Bethel Bible Institute regarding the
Dudley Hill properties were made to the Nichols Academy Board of Trustees
in late 1922. A representative of the Bethel Bible Institute had been attending a
convention at the Conant Memorial Church when he responded to questions
about the Institute's future by inquiring about the availability of Academy
buildings. Apparently Bethel was looking to expand, but was limited in
Spencer by "outgrown quarters," a need for new buildings, and rundown
equipment. Nichols Academy was seen by the Bethel Bible Institute's
representative as an ideal facility at a perfect location.[42]

The Bethel Bible Institute prepared a formal request to the Nichols Academy Board between October and December 1922. The Spencer institution wanted to acquire or lease the Conant Mansion house (Budleigh Hall), the farm and buildings on the Conant estate, and the three school buildings then comprising Nichols Academy: the Academy building, the former Conant dormitory or Dudley Inn, and Conant Library. The Bethel Bible Institute's application indicated that its proposed school in Dudley would function as it had been doing in Spencer. The new institution, like the old institute, was to be interdenominational and focus on training for Bible and Christian service, as well as continuing to combine work and study from which students were to receive "a practical working knowledge of essential pursuits and the essentials of learning." Bethel supporters stated that its school would offer secondary school subjects for Dudley students, keep the library open for the townspeople of Dudley, have rooms in the inn available for visitors during the school year, and open the entire inn to visitors for two summer months.[43]

To avoid misunderstandings and counter possible local criticism, Reverend Goodell, as the president of the Nichols Academy Board of Trustees, carefully spelled out the reasoning behind leasing the Academy buildings to the Bethel Bible Institute. In his March 1923, letter to the *Webster Times*, he wrote:

> . . . it [the Academy building] has only performed the function of a junior high school for the town. The Trustees felt that there was a larger field of usefulness for it. . . . We became convinced that this school [Bethel Bible Institute] would perpetuate the purposes of Nichols Academy in a far better way than could be accomplished by any other plan we had in mind. . . . We believe that this arrangement will be of great value to the town of Dudley. It will introduce an element of culture and training, which will affect for good the entire life of the town and make our hill-top once more a place where eager and devoted students will come to fit themselves for a great life's work.[44]

A primary reason for the Academy's acceptance of the Bethel Bible Institute's offer, according to Reverend Goodell, was the support given to this idea by Morris Conant, grandson of Hezekiah Conant, who was acting for the Conant estate. After some deliberations, the estate indicated its willingness to transfer Budleigh Hall and the adjacent former Conant property to the Bethel Bible Institute for "$1.00."[45] This was a tempting opportunity for the Spencer institution. The Academy trustees, when they learned of the decision of the Conant estate, became "more inclined" to lease their buildings.[46]

Founded in 1900, the Bethel Bible Institute had been incorporated in 1909. According to its constitution, its objectives included "the teaching of the Bible for the purpose of Evangelism, Bible Teaching, Missionary, pastoral and Sunday School Work, also instruction in such secular branches of study as shall be required to equip the students for whichever of these lines of work the Lord shall lead them to do."[47] Its founder and president, Essek William Kenyon, a Free Will Baptist, had an enthusiastic following as a widely known evangelist, pastor, and author.

Unique in many ways, the Spencer institution provided a free education to any Christian young man or woman. Its teachers received no salaries. In turn, students worked four hours each day to support themselves and their institution. The Bethel Bible Institute taught a full range of courses and subjects from elementary school to college preparatory courses. Over time it had gained significant support from numerous well-wishers for refusing to let hardships such as a lack of many modern conveniences interfere with the development of its educational program.[48] Prior to World War I, the Spencer school had grown to 50 students but declined shortly thereafter.[49] Its 200 or so graduates were scattered throughout the world as missionaries, ministers, and other professionals.

Not everyone supported the move of the Bethel Bible Institute to Dudley Hill. Some disliked the Institute's evangelistic approach and disagreed with Reverend Goodell and the Nichols trustees. They believed its presence would upset many longstanding local relationships. Others felt that the Bible School's contribution was not going to help the Dudley community. One of the most aggressive opponents of the Institute's move to Dudley was Samuel Morris Conant, Hezekiah's son, and the father of Morris Conant. He predicted that the coming of the school would "drive many people from the town. . . ." The arrival of the Bethel Bible Institute, as he saw it, was "an attack from the outside" that would upset the traditions of Nichols Academy and establish a "small religious cult on Dudley Hill."[50] Samuel Morris Conant was opposed to what he saw as "sectarian education," and what he felt had been absent from Dudley Hill for many years. The Bethel Bible Institute, in response, challenged this criticism claiming that "all fanaticism and fads have been eliminated from [its] school life. . . ."[51] Nonetheless, this argument resulted in a serious and unfortunate rift in the Conant family and, to a lesser extent, in the greater Dudley community.[52]

Certain conditions had to be met by the Bethel Bible Institute before Nichols Academy would lease its four buildings (Nichols Academy building, Conant Library and Observatory, the Conant Inn, and its stable). For one, the Bible Institute had to raise $25,000 in gifts or pledges to demonstrate its ability to maintain the property. This was done within several months.[53] The Spencer school also had to agree to offer instruction in language, liberal arts and sciences "and other branches of learning in conformity with the act of the General Assembly of Massachusetts, June 18, 1819," which had established Nichols Academy. This made it possible for local students to take subjects at the Dudley Bible School and complete their secondary school education.

In the process, the Academy trustees' commitment to the Universalist-designed curriculum and to Amasa Nichols' vision of a school on Dudley Hill had been steadfast. Its terms were accepted by the Bethel Bible Institute. The Nichols Academy Board of Trustees had kept Hezekiah Conant's promise to the town that Conant Library was to be available to the Dudley community by requiring that the new institution keep it open every afternoon. Conant Hall, or the Dudley Inn, also was to be open to furnish meals "at a reasonable charge" and operated as a hotel during July and August. The Academy also wanted its buildings available for local meetings, reunions, and other occasions. And, finally, the Bethel Bible Institute agreed to change its name to the "Dudley Bible Institute and Nichols Academy."[54] This newly-named institution formally leased the four Academy buildings at the top of the Hill on February 24, 1923, and then acquired ownership of the Conant estate. This was an important although a generally overlooked step which essentially established the general dimensions of an eventual college campus that followed in 1931.[55]

Within a year, President Kenyon of the Bethel Bible Institute left for the west coast and soon was replaced by Howard W. Ferrin. This must have been difficult for the former Spencer institute since President Kenyon had been with the institution for twenty years and was extremely well known. Then too, the relationship between the Academy and the Bethel Bible Institute was not entirely satisfactory. In September 1925, Reverend Goodell felt compelled to write to Reverend Paul Rader, a leading evangelist then assisting the Bible Institute. Goodell reminded him that the Dudley Bible Institute needed to appreciate "the attitude of the Trustees when I tell you that Mr. Conant named the hall [in the Academy building] 'Alumni Hall' and wanted it always to be used for the community." Apparently this was not happening. Reverend Goodell strongly urged Reverend Rader to have the Inn ready for transients and summer guests for the benefit of the local community. He also recommended that cordial relations with the First Congregational Church be maintained.[56]

The leased Academy buildings on the west side of the main road were returned by the Dudley Bible Institute to Nichols Academy the following fall. Formal minutes of trustee meetings in 1926 note only that the Academy was putting its buildings back in the "same condition" that they had been in when originally leased to the Dudley Bible Institute.[57] Perhaps the Dudley Bible Institute no longer believed that the buildings leased from the Academy were worth the required investment. Possibly the ideals of the Academy as embodied in its agreement with the Bethel Bible Institute were too restrictive for the Bethel Bible Institute as it began to expand. There can be little question, judging from the finality involved, that both parties agreed to end the lease.

After 1926, the "Dudley Bible Institute," formerly the "Dudley Bible Institute and Nichols Academy," and before that the Bethel Bible Institute, operated only in the buildings of the former Hezekiah Conant Estate. This institution was headquartered in Budleigh Hall and remained on Dudley Hill until 1929 when it left for Providence, Rhode Island. After several moves in Rhode Island, the then Providence-Barrington College merged with Gordon College of Wenham, Massachusetts, in 1985. As for the now unused former Conant estate and the Academy buildings, an observant reporter wrote in December 1929 that the buildings on Dudley Hill were empty and "the entire town is in a state of slumber."[58] This lasted only for a brief period.

With the Bible Institute out of its hill top buildings (although still occupying the former Conant estate), the Academy again was confronted by Dudley parties regarding the 1871 Dudley-Academy agreement and town use of the Academy building.[59] In this fifty-year-old agreement, the Academy originally had agreed to allow the town use of the Academy building if classes were not being held by the Academy. Discussions and town meetings during the years following 1909 considered some options. However, little was settled as the town continued using the Academy building as a junior high school until 1923.

When the Dudley Bible Institute gave up the leased buildings in 1926, the Academy trustees offered the Academy building to the town along with land.[60] The only formal town reaction to this proposal, however, was from the Dudley school committee that concluded it would be "wise" for Dudley to continue sending high school pupils to Webster and Southbridge rather than to incur expenses surrounding the construction and maintenance of a high school in Dudley.[61] This recommendation was consistent with their conclusions and reports over the previous fifteen years.[62] Discussions ended when the Academy rescinded its decision to offer the Academy building to the town.[63] The full responsibility for the future of the Conant legacy again was in the hands of the Nichols Academy Board of Trustees.

This refocused their attention to the buildings on Academy Row. Repairs always were necessary as the trustees sought to maintain relations with the community. The trustees agreed to allow town boys free use of Academy Hall (probably for basketball) and to make Academy Hall available for community activities.[64] This included the offer of the Academy building to the town for a high school, which the trustees then rescinded.

Much time and money was spent on refurbishing Academy buildings for further use between 1926 and 1931. In 1927 alone, $6,439.62 was spent on the repairs for the Inn and $623.61 for the Library.[65] The search for someone to lease the campus continued without much success. Some inquiries were rejected as being "unsuited." Letters asking for assistance were sent by the Academy trustees to educational consultant Porter Sargent of Boston, but went unanswered at first.[66] And, in September 1929, Reverend Goodell resigned as president of the trustees after 53 years as an Academy trustee.[67]

But the passage of time and the nature of the Academy's existence had put its trustees in a difficult position. Its buildings had to be used for educational purposes while being made available to the townspeople of Dudley as originally determined by Hezekiah Conant or stated in the property deeds for the Conant land and buildings. For instance, the Library and the Inn were to be returned to the Conant family if not used for educational functions and were, with the Academy Hall, to be kept open for the community. It appears that the Dudley Bible Institute had not paid as much attention to these issues as the Nichols Academy trustees believed necessary. Possibly Academy trustee conditions had not been realistic. Regardless, by 1930, these buildings needed repairs and continuous staffing without producing much income. The Academy also managed its investments of about $30,000 in securities with nearly $10,000 of that designated for student scholarships (the Hancock, Congdon, and Conant Funds).[68] Two potential users of these buildings, the town and the Dudley Bible Institute, either had not wanted the old buildings or, as in the case of the Bible Institute, could not agree on appropriate terms. Some members of the Nichols Academy Board of Trustees inquired if they could sell Nichols Academy. This question went unanswered for some time. At the same moment, the Great Depression was entering its second year and its impact was beginning to limit expansive planning. To their great credit, the trustees stuck to their task, although it appears they were becoming frustrated and alarmed.

A NEW HAMPSHIRE JUNIOR COLLEGE PROGRAM

A creditable inquiry regarding the leasing of Academy property came in early 1931 from a preparatory school in central New Hampshire. Discussions quickly advanced between a Nichols Academy trustee committee led by Dr. Quincy H. Merrill and two administrators from the New Hampton School in New Hampton, New Hampshire: Headmaster Frederick Smith and his assistant, James L. Conrad.[69] Dr. Merrill and his Academy trustee colleagues were impressed by the success of the New Hampton Junior College of Business Administration program which had been in operation for several years at the New Hampshire preparatory school. Smith and Conrad wanted to relocate their junior college program. During a relatively brief but aggressive negotiating period set up with the assistance of Porter Sargent of Boston, an agreement was reached on March 24, 1931.[70] The announcement of James L. Conrad's election to the presidency of Nichols Junior College of Business Administration and Executive Training was made on April 1, 1931.[71]

There can be little question that the Academy representatives had understood they had to create a more acceptable and viable campus. Furthermore, they learned from their experience with the Bethel Bible Institute that all arrangements had to be clearly stated. What they did not know, they were told by Smith and Conrad, both experienced and successful educators, who had just restructured the New Hampton School. Dr. Merrill's Academy committee also had contacted the managers and trustees of the Bible Institute regarding the availability of the former Conant estate.

The Academy trustees, probably at the request of Smith and Conrad, sought to bring the land and buildings of the former Conant estate together with those of the Academy as the Bethel Bible Institute originally had done and thus develop a complete campus. Most of the eight buildings located on the two campus areas had to be renovated and remodeled. Athletic fields and other facilities had to be constructed for the new college. Then too, land issues with the town dealing with the Dudley Inn area had to be resolved by Nichols Academy and several small mortgages eliminated.[72] In all, these renovations and campus improvements were expected to cost Nichols Academy at least $14,000, although some estimates went as high as $40,000. Fortunately, the years since its closing had seen Academy investments grow with some success.

After a flurry of activity, the Academy trustees met on April 21, 1931, to vote on an agreement with the two New Hampshire educators. First, the Merrill Committee had to acquire the former Conant estate. In their earlier discussion with the Dudley Bible Institute, apparently the Academy agreed to pay $5,000 for the Conant estate contingent on its ability to mortgage the Budleigh Hall property.[73] It also was agreed that the Bible Institute could stay in the former Conant estate until August 9, 1931.

Led by Dr. Quincy Merrill and his Academy committee, Nichols Academy trustees approved the lease for the Academy property, including the Budleigh Hall land and buildings about to be acquired by the Academy. This lease to James L. Conrad and Frederick Smith was for five years beginning July 1, 1931, at a yearly rental of $1,500.00, with an option for an additional twenty-five years. The board then appointed one of its members, George Hall, to oversee what was being spent on the property. Lastly, they appealed through the Probate Court system to have the resources of the Congdon and Hancock Scholarship Funds made available for building repairs.[74] Within two months, $8,000 from these funds, including the Conant Fund, was approved by the Probate Court for improvements to the Academy's buildings.

A final part of this agreement was completed when Nichols Academy acquired the former Conant estate from the former Bethel Bible Institute for five thousand dollars in late July, 1931.[75] This move made the agreement with Smith and Conrad final. Importantly, it brought together two major parcels of land on Dudley Hill under the Academy's ownership. This was to be the campus leased by Smith and Conrad and soon to function as Nichols Junior College of Business Administration and Executive Training.

In September, the trustees of Nichols Academy formally approved the lease for the original Academy property and the just-acquired former Conant estate to Frederick Smith and James L. Conrad for Nichols Junior College of Business Administration and Executive Training. The College opened on September 21, 1931. In the process, the Academy trustees agreed to assume the expense of the library and to make sure that it was open for the citizens of Dudley as Hezekiah Conant had intended. It was also agreed that Academy Hall was to be available to the citizens of Dudley when needed. Clearly the Academy trustees were making every effort not to make the mistakes they had made in the earlier agreement with the Bethel Bible Institute.

Some things, however, could not change. As they had done with the Bethel Bible Institute, the Nichols Academy trustees insisted that the commitment to Amasa Nichols' vision be continued. Smith and Conrad agreed that this property was to be used "in conformity with the Charter of Nichols Academy," thereby establishing a somewhat vague, but nonetheless a very real "tie" between the two institutions.[76] The fact that the new college was functioning in buildings and on property still owned and managed by the old Academy was another.

Leasing the Academy buildings, including the former Conant estate, to Nichols Junior College in 1931 did not mean the end of the Nichols Academy Board of Trustees. This group continued to function as the manager of remaining Academy funds and owner of the campus land and buildings leased by Nichols Junior College. This was to be a challenging and often perplexing arrangement. In effect, Nichols Academy and the new junior college had become informal affiliates in a new educational undertaking. One owned the land and buildings; the other provided the educational direction and substance. Nonetheless, the educational institution that had been established by Amasa Nichols essentially had come to an end. The Nichols Academy Board of Trustees had done its work well. The trustees were rightly congratulated by a local newspaper for "effecting the transfer of a successful school [program]" like the New Hampton Junior College of Business Administration.[77] The Nichols Academy owned campus and buildings eventually would be sold by its trustees to Nichols Junior College in 1942.[78]

Nichols Academy had begun in 1815 to educate a rural population and it did – at least three generations of young men and women. Although small, rural, and poorly funded for a good part of its early years, the Academy had been a transforming force. Those who attended the Academy benefited greatly.

Young men were given the opportunity to move beyond their rural villages and up through the new society's social ranks due to academic backgrounds they received at the Academy. Young women demonstrated their abilities and acquired a greater awareness of the world around them. This was what their families had wanted. The Academy also tested educational methods and models for public schools to follow. If there was any loss, it was experienced by the small, rural town of Dudley that saw some of its best and most aggressive minds moving away. Some, such as Hezekiah Conant and Reverend Charles Goodell, returned, but they were the exceptions. Perhaps the biggest gainer was an American society that benefited from talents that would not have been available if it had not been for academies such as Nichols.

The Dudley Hill academy had emerged from under the shadow of the American Revolution as the Latin grammar school decreased in popularity. The rise of the small, rural academy introduced a new era that saw a broader, more expansive, more middle class oriented educational institution that offered support for more practical educational needs while still concerned with the requirements of an educational elite. This is what had made it special. The ability to provide a secondary school education for a wider number of people with practical needs as well as lofty ambitions functioned as a splendid combination for nearly a century. In the process, the Universalist Academy was replaced by "old" Nichols Academy, in turn by Mr. Conant's Academy.

After the Civil War, pressures from previously supporting elements – college interests and state government – began to dominate the directions and content of secondary education. Nichols Academy served both as the town's high school and as a college preparatory school. While the popular acceptance of a "fitting for college was the same as fitting for life" philosophy was not long-lived, Nichols Academy had to deal with this thinking at a point in time when it was not appropriate for a declining Dudley academy faced with the results of a shifting local population.[79] In 1909 the Academy stopped admitting students; only eight had enrolled for the next year.

By 1920, the nature of secondary schooling was being aggressively debated. Social efficiency, not mental training or intellectual development, was about to become the primary focus of a coming era. The pedagogical core of the emerging comprehensive high school shifted away from the exclusive development of the intellect and toward the need to make a living that involved gathering information rather than training the mind. Social control and social efficiency soon would become forces behind the comprehensive high school.[80] Nichols Academy was not to be involved. Its time had passed.

The Nichols Academy story presents a remarkable example of a firm and enduring commitment that encompassed both space and vision. It had been a splendid journey that touched the lives of many people. But this is not the end of the story. On September 21, 1931, the "spring on the hill" began to flow again. Amasa Nichols' vision was about to move to its next stage in the form of Nichols Junior College of Business Administration and Executive Training. The Nichols Academy Trustees had succeeded in bringing the dream of Amasa Nichols into the 20th Century.

Endnotes

Introduction

1. "Exercises," *Graduation and Re-union of Alumni, Nichols Academy, 1886, 1887, 1888* (Webster: John Cort, Printer, 1888), 20, Nichols College Archives, Nichols College, Dudley, Massachusetts (hereafter cited NCA).

2. One of the few to mention Nichols Academy in a general study of New England academies is Harriet Webster Marr, *The Old New England Academies; Founded Before 1826* (New York: Comet Press Books, 1959), 5, 295. Historians of Universalism, in discussing the Universalists' efforts to establish an educational institution, focus on their difficulties during the first four years of Nichols Academy's existence. For interesting discussions of this brief stage in Nichols Academy's history, see Russell E. Miller, *A Light on the Hill: A History of Tufts College, 1852–1952* (Boston: Beacon Press, 1966); Richard Eddy, *Universalism in America*, 2 Vols. (Boston: Universalist Publishing House, 1884–1886); Thomas Whittemore, *The Modern History of Universalism* (Boston: by the author, 40 Cornhill, 1830). Otherwise, the Academy is sometimes included in brief introductions to the present-day Nichols College. Refer to Darcy C. Coyle, *Nichols College: A Brief History* (New York: Newcomen Society in America, 1975). For a comparison of Nichols Academy with nearby Woodstock Academy in Woodstock, Connecticut, founded in 1801, see Robert John Smith, "The Survival of an Old New England Academy: Secondary Education in Woodstock, Connecticut, 1801–1971," Ph.D. diss., University of Connecticut, 1986. For a recent assessment of an early academy experience, see J. M. Opal, "Exciting Emulation: Academies and the Transformation of the Rural North, 1780s–1820s," *Journal of American History* 91 (September 2004): 460–463.

3. This is also the conclusion of Stuart G. Noble, *A History of American Education*, rev. ed. (New York: Holt, Rinehart and Winston, 1961), 34.

4. Timothy Dwight, *Travels in New England and New York*, (New Haven, 1821) I:37, quoted in Richard G. Durnin, "New England's Eighteenth Century's Incorporated Academies: Their Origin and Development to 1850," Ph.D. diss., University of Pennsylvania, 1968, 38.

5. Elwood P. Cubberley, *Public Education in the United States: A Study and Interpretation of American Educational History* (Boston and New York: Houghton Mifflin Company, 1934), 247.

6. *Granite State Monthly*, 1887, quoted in Marr, *Old New England Academies*, 293.

7. Marr, *Old New England Academies*, 294. For another important study of early academies, see Durnin, "New England's Eighteenth Century Incorporated Academies."

8. Bradford Academy became Bradford Junior College in 1932 and Bradford College in 1971. Bradford closed in 2000. Leicester Academy became Leicester Junior College in 1954 merging with Becker College in 1977. Only Nichols continues as an independent Massachusetts college with a direct connection to its 1815 origins. Nichols experienced a number of name changes: From Nichols Academy to Nichols Junior College of Business Administration and Executive Training (1931) to Nichols College of Business Administration (1958) and to Nichols College (1971).

9. Charles L. Goodell, *Black Tavern Tales: Stories of Old New England* (Brooklyn, N.Y.: Willis McDonald & Co., 1932), 29.

10. Durnin, "New England's Eighteenth Century's Incorporated Academies," 2.

11. Noble, *A History of American Education*, 112–134.

12. Elmer Ellsworth Brown, *The Making of Our Middle Schools; An account of the Development of Secondary Education in the United States* (New York: Longmans, Green, 1903), 228.

13. Ibid., 228–255. Also see Cubberley, *Public Education in the United States*, 245–255; R. Freeman Butts, Lawrence A. Cremin, *A History of Education in American Culture* (New York: Henry Holt and Company, 1953), 250–253; Joseph Murphy, et al, *The Productive High School: Creating Personalized Academic Communities* (Thousand Oaks, Calif.: Corwin Press, Inc., 2001), 4–6, 22–23.

14. Theodore R. Sizer, "The Academies: An Interpretation," in *The Age of the Academies*, ed. Theodore R. Sizer (New York: Columbia University, 1964), 5–6.

15. Michael B. Katz, *Class, Bureaucracy, and Schools: The Illusion of Educational Change in America* (New York: Prager Publishers, 1971), xv.

16. Ibid. xviii. Katz believes that corporate voluntarism with an aggressive academy-building ability emerged in the early nineteenth century to take the lead. Unfortunately, this surge only served to bring out the inherent weaknesses in this approach such as limited funds, the tendency to promote disharmony in an industrial age, an undemocratic nature, and the inability of parents to control their children's education. As a result, this "corporate voluntarism" model was replaced by an "incipient bureaucracy" model which then came to dominate educational thinking.

17. Marr, *Old New England Academies*, 287–296; Durnin, "New England's Eighteenth Century's Incorporated Academies," 81.

18. James McLachlan, *American Boarding Schools: A Historical Study* (New York: Charles Scribner's Sons, 1970), 193.

CHAPTER 1 ~ THE FIRST ACADEMY: A DISCORDANT BEGINNING, 1815–1823

1. Carl F. Kaestle, *Pillars of the Republic: Common School and American Society, 1780–1860* (New York: Hill and Wang, 1983), 102.

2. Cubberley, *Public Education in the United States*, 247.

3. Albert E. Van Dusen, *Connecticut* (New York: Random House, 1961), 348–349.

4. Cubberley, *Public Education in the United States*, 247, 259.

5. Durnin, "New England's Eighteenth-Century Incorporated Academies," 42.

6. Gordon S. Wood, "Significance of the Early Republic," *Journal of the Early Republic*, 8 (Spring 1988): 18.

7. Steven E. Tozer, Paul C. Violas, and Guy Senese, *School and Society: Historical and Contemporary Perspectives*, 3rd ed. (New York: McGraw-Hill Primis Custom Publishing, 1998), 52–53.

8. Cubberley, *Public Education in the United States*, 61–63.

9. Harlan Updegraff, *The Origin of the Moving School in Massachusetts* (New York: Columbia University Press, 1907).

10. Emit Duncan Grizzell, *Origin and Development of the High School in New England before 1865* (Philadelphia: the Macmillan Company, 1923), 28–29.

11. Benjamin Franklin, quoted in R. Freeman Butts and Lawrence A. Cremin, *A History of Education in American Culture* (New York: Henry Holt and Company, 1953), 78–79.

12. Reverend James H. Francis, "'Copy of a Discourse,' Delivered on Fast-Day, April 9, 1835, containing an Historical Sketch of the town of Dudley, Mass." in *A Souvenir of the Conant Memorial Church; Its Inception, Construction, and Dedication* (Boston: Printed for Hezekiah Conant by Forbes Lithograph Manufacturing Company, 1893), 83.

13. *Commemorative Biographical Record of Tolland and Windham Counties, Connecticut; containing biographical sketches of prominent and representative citizens of the early settled families* (Chicago: J. H. Beers, 1903), 192; Dudley Town Meeting Minutes, May 7, 1792, *Town Records of Dudley, Massachusetts, 1754–1794* (Pawtucket, R.I.: The Adam Sutcliffe Co., 1894), 363.

14. Robert J. Stets, preparer, *Postmasters and Postoffices of the United States 1702–1811* (Lake Oswego, Oregon: LaPasta Publication, 1994), 146.

15. *Dudley Town Meeting Records 1794–1845*, microfilm, FHL 861113, Genealogical Society of Utah, Salt Lake City, 1971, 180.

16. Refer to Worcester County Registry of Deeds, Worcester Court House, Worcester, Mass., Deed Books 147:561; 147:562; 162:510; 164:331; 164:336–337; 172:253; 172:584; 175:282; 183:286; 185:552; 186:504; 186:506; 186:507; 188:48–50; 188:343; 188:382; 198:284; 198:429.

17. The best place to begin with the Amasa Nichols story is with Holmes Ammidown, a student at the Academy in 1820 from nearby Southbridge, who later became a careful scholar and local historian. His father was a member of the first Nichols Academy Board of Trustees. Holmes Ammidown's *Historical Collections* (N.Y.: by the author, 1874), I:430–431, is a primary source for information on the early Academy and Amasa Nichols.

18. *National Aegis*, April 15, 1816.

19. For this projection, see http://www.austintxgensoc.org/calculatecpi.html.

20. For other early academies, see Durnin, "New England's Eighteenth Century Incorporated Academies," 124–125.

21. Russell E. Miller, *The Larger Hope: The First Century of the Universalist Church in America, 1710–1870* (Boston: Unitarian Universalist Association, 1979), 371.

22. Ammidown, *Historical Collections*, I:424–425.

23. Worcester County Registry of Deeds, Worcester, Mass., 209:646–647; 210:240.

24. D. Hamilton Hurd, *History of Worcester County, Massachusetts* (Philadelphia: J.W. Lewis & Co., 1889) II:1364, 1365; *Catalogue . . . Nichols Academy . . . 1855–56*, 11, NCA.

25. *Universalist Magazine*, October 5, 1822, 59.

26. Michael G. Kenny, *The Perfect Law of Liberty: Elias Smith and the Providential History of America* (Washington and London: Smithsonian Institution Press, 1994), 60–88; Russell E. Miller, *A Light on the Hill: A History of Tufts College, 1852–1952* (Boston: Beacon Press, 1966), 4–5.

27. Robert A. Ferguson, *The American Enlightenment, 1750–1820* (Cambridge, Mass.: Harvard University Press, 1997), 22–43; Durnin, "New England's Eighteenth Century Incorporated Academies," 73, 152.

28. Ernest Cassara, *Universalism in America: A Documentary History* (Boston: Beacon Kress, 1971), 5. For the best discussion of the Universalists' early involvement in education, see Miller, *A Light on the Hill*, 5–6.

29. Ernest Cassara, *Hosea Ballou, The Challenge to Orthodoxy* (Washington, D.C.: University Press of America, Inc., 1982), 16–17.

30. Ann Lee Bressler, *The Universalist Movement in America, 1770–1880* (Oxford and New York: Oxford University Press, 2001), 148.

31. Ibid., 158.

32. Clinton Lee Scott, *The Universalist Church in America; a Short History* (Boston: Universalist Historical Society, 1957), 77.

33. Russell E. Miller, *A Light On The Hill*, 8–9.

34. Thomas Whittemore, *The Modern History of Universalism* (Boston: Cornhill, 1830), 376. Eddy, *Universalism in America*, I:411. At a Nichols Academy graduation in 1882, Academy Trustee Clark Jillson stated that the Academy had its beginnings in 1814 in Westmoreland, New Hampshire. See *Eighth Annual Reunion of the Alumni, Nichols Academy. June 16, 1882*, 24, NCA.

35. Whittemore, *Modern History of Universalism*, 377.

36. Nichols Academy Cash Book, May 24, 1819, NCA.

37. Ibid., May 24, 1819 – August 16, 1819, NCA.

38. Cubberley, *Public Education in the United States*, 248.

39. Laws of Massachusetts, May 1819 – February 1822, Chap. CLV, June 18, 1819, 242; Ammidown, *Historical Collections*, I:425–26; *Charter and Constitution of Nichols Academy* (Pawtucket, R.I.: The Adam Sutcliffe Co., 1897); Durnin, "New England's Eighteenth Century's Incorporated Academies," 253–286. One academy, Bristol Academy in Taunton, Massachusetts, added an additional dimension stating its purpose was to "promote piety, morality, and patriotism."

40. Refer also to Durnin, "New England's Eighteenth Century's Incorporated Academies," 111.

41. Worcester County Registry of Deeds, Worcester, Massachusetts, Amasa Nichols to Nichols Academy Trustees, August 7, 1819, 218:44–45.

42. Nichols Academy Board of Trustees Meeting Minutes, August 11, 1819, NCA.

43. Eddy, *Universalism in America*, 412. According to Russell E. Miller, Eddy's work provides the "most comprehensive and detailed coverage of American Universalism." See Miller, *Light on the Hill*, 5, n. 2; Whittemore, *Modern History of Universalism*, 376–378.

44. *Universalist Magazine*, I, December 4, 1819, 89.

45. *Proceedings of the General Convention of the New England States and others . . .*, September 14, 1819, microfilm, Shaw & Shoemaker, 49963; *Constitution of Nichols Academy*, 1819, NCA.

46. For a list of these institutions, see Clinton Lee Scott, *The Universalist Church in America: A Short History* (Boston: Universalist Historical Society, 1957), 76–78.

47. In a letter to Reverend Edward Turner in Charlestown, Amasa Nichols asked him to refer his letter to "Doct. Thompson, Esq. Gleason, Esq. Kettell and B. Russell" suggesting that they probably came from the Boston area. See copy of letter, Amasa Nichols to Rev. Edward Turner, May 1, 1821, Folder 2400, NCA. (Original is in Edward Turner Papers, bMS 101, box 2, folder 21. Andover-Harvard Theological Library, Harvard Divinity School, Harvard University, Cambridge, Massachusetts, and is being used with permission of the Andover-Harvard Theological Library.)

48. "*Constitution of Nichols Academy, 1819*," NCA.

49. Ibid. This phrase also can be found in the *Constitution of Phillips Academy in Andover* (1778)," quoted in Sizer, *The Age of the Academies*, 86.

50. Article Six, *Constitution of Nichols Academy, Dudley, 1819*.

51. Cassara, *Hosea Ballou: The Challenge to Orthodoxy*, 158.

52. Smith, *Religious Education in Massachusetts*, 122.

53. See *Constitution of Nichols Academy, 1819*, NCA.

54. For instance, see "An Oration delivered at the Meeting House in Dudley, Mass., Tuesday, February 28, 1815, on the celebration of peace" (Worcester, Mass.: Henry Rogers, 1815). Richard Carrique is identified as the pastor of the Universalist Societies of Charlton, Oxford and Dudley.

55. For Samuel Slater's role, see Jonathan Prude, *The Coming of Industrial Order: Town and Life in Rural Massachusetts, 1810–1860* (Cambridge: Cambridge University Press, 1983), 49–64, 271; Barbara M. Tucker, *Samuel Slater and the Origins of the American Textile Industry, 1790–1860* (Ithaca and London: Cornell University Press, 1984), 126. Also see James L. Conrad Jr., "The Establishment of the Textile Industry in Dudley, Massachusetts, 1812–1820," master's thesis, Clark University, 1963; Paul J. Macek and James R. Morrison, *Early History of Webster, Dudley, and Oxford* (Webster, Mass.: by Paul J. Macek and James R. Morrison, 2000), 215–223.

56. Goodell, *Black Tavern Tales*, 29.

57. Copy of letter, Amasa Nichols to Edward Turner, May 1, 1821, NCA. (Original is in Andover-Harvard Theological Library, Harvard Divinity School, Cambridge, Mass.)

58. Robert John Smith, "The Survival of an Old New England Academy: Secondary Education in Woodstock, Connecticut, 1801–1971," Ph.D. diss., University of Connecticut, 1986, 69.

59. Henry L. Canfield, quoted in Russell E. Miller, *The Larger Hope*, 365.

NICHOLS ACADEMY: THE SPRING ON THE HILL ∽

60. Universalist Church *Proceedings*, September 14–15, 1819, microfilm, Shaw & Shoemaker: 49963.

61. Claude M. Fuess, *An Old New England School: A History of Phillips Academy* (Boston: Houghton Mifflin Company, 1917), 67.

62. Ammidown, *Historical Collections*, I:425–429.

63. Nichols Academy Board of Trustees Meeting Minutes, August 11, 1819, NCA.

64. Ibid.

65. Ibid., August 23, 1820, NCA; Ibid., August 22, 1821; Ibid., April 10, 1822; Ibid., June 12, 1822; Ibid., October 30, 1822.

66. Ibid., October 30, 1822; Ibid., November–January, 1822–1823.

67. Ibid., May 24, 1820.

68. Ibid., August 23, 1820.

69. Philo Academicus, in *Universalist Magazine*, March 18, 1820, I:151.

70. Cassara, *Universalism in America*, 25–27; Bressler, *The Universalist Movement in America, 1770–1880*, 42.

71. Worcester County Registry of Deeds, Amasa Nichols to Samuel Slater, November 29, 1821, 266:414; Ibid., September 13, 1823, 235:74; Ibid, November 10, 1824, 241:177.

72. Copy of letter, Nichols to Turner, May 1, 1821, NCA. (The original is in the Andover-Harvard Theological Library, Harvard Divinity School, Cambridge, Mass.)

73. Ibid. Also see *Proceedings of the General Convention of the New England States and others . . .* , September 14–15, 1819, microfilm, Shaw & Shoemaker: 49963.

74. See Ammidown, *Historical Collections*, I:430–431.

75. Nichols Academy Board of Trustee Meeting Minutes, January 6, 1823, NCA.

76. Worcester County Registry of Deeds, Worcester, Massachusetts, Amasa Nichols to William Winsor, September 28, 1826, 251:509; Amasa Nichols to William Jewell, December 31, 1827, 260:8–10.

77. Miller, *Light On The Hill*, 9.

78. Holmes Ammidown, *Historical Collections*, I:430–431.

79. Nichols Academy Board of Trustees Meeting Minutes, November 17, 1824, NCA.

80. In what appears to be a related development in 1871, the Nichols Academy Board of Trustees requested that Frederick Nichols, Juliet Nichols, and Sarah Newman, release Academy trustees from any claims as the heirs of Amasa Nichols. They agreed. No further details are included in this agreement, but this may have referred to Amasa Nichols' possible claim on the Academy property. Refer to Worcester County Registry of Deeds, Worcester, Mass., 850:284. Also see Registry of Deeds, 218:44–45.

81. Francis, "Discourse," 83.

82. Ibid., 84.

83. Joshua Bates, D.D., "Topographical and Historical Notices of the Town of Dudley, Mass." in *An Anniversary Discourse, Delivered at Dudley, Mass., March 20, 1853* (Boston: T.R. Marvin, 42 Congress Street, 1853), 56.

84. *Constitution of Nichols Academy, 1819*. NCA.

85. Reverend Goodell to Editor, *Webster Times*, March 13, 1923.

86. *Webster Times*, June 24, 1881.

CHAPTER 2 ~ THE OLD ACADEMY IN OPERATION, 1823–1860

1. Cubberley, *Public Education in the United States*, 14.

2. Ibid., 17.

3. Ammidown, *Historical Collections*, II:337.

4. Cubberley, *Public Education in the United States*, 289, n. 1.

5. Noble, *History of American Education*, 131–132.

6. *Charter and Constitution of Nichols Academy, Dudley, Mass., with notes from its records* (Pawtucket, R.I.: The Adam Sutcliffe Co., 1897), 27.

7. Cubberley, *Public Education in the United States*, 257. Also see Updegraff, *Origin of the Moving School in Massachusetts*, 170.

8. Marr, *Old New England Academies*, 289.

9. Grizzell, *Origin and Development of the High School in New England*, 86–87.

10. Nichols Academy Board of Trustees Meeting Minutes, February 20, 1828, NCA. Dudley Town Meeting Minutes, April 7, 1828, microfilm FHL 861113, Genealogical Society of Utah, Salt Lake City, Utah, 1971.

11. Entries, 1827–1828, Nichols Academy Cash Book, 1819–1829, NCA.

12. These figures report individual enrollments for each term with four terms a year. In some cases, if students stayed more than one term, they then were counted twice or more. See Nichols Academy Cash Book, 1819–1828, NCA.

13. Account of Boarding, Nichols Academy, 1822–1828, NCA.

14. Copy of letter, Nichols to Turner, May 1, 1821, NCA.

15. This list of towns represented by student enrollments (with the student numbers in parentheses) included Dudley (37), Oxford (12), Thompson in Connecticut (4), Charlton (6), Barstow (1), Woodstock in Connecticut (11), Rhode Island (1), Sutton (3), Southbridge (9), Pomfret in Connecticut (2), Pawtucket in Rhode Island (1), Smithfield in Rhode Island (1), Uxbridge (3). Refer to Entries, 1826–1827, Nichols Academy Cash Book, 1819–1828, NCA.

16. Copy of letter, Amasa Nichols to Turner, May 1, 1821, NCA.

17. Nichols Academy Cash Book, 1827–1828, NCA. These enrollment figures are only based on enrollment for the fall, winter, and spring terms. The summer term or terms are not included.

18. Nichols Academy Board of Trustees Meeting Minutes, February 20, 1828, NCA; Ibid., March 24, 1829.

19. *Catalogue . . . Nichols Academy . . .1835*, NCA.

20. *Constitution of Nichols Academy, 1819*, NCA.

21. *Nichols (College) Budget*, October 21, 1939, NCA; *Catalogue . . . Nichols Academy, Dudley, Mass., 1841*, 6, NCA.

22. *Catalogue . . . Nichols Academy, 1845*, NCA.

23. Nichols Academy Board of Trustees Meeting Minutes, September 5, 1837, NCA; *Catalogue . . .Nichols Academy . . . 1835*, NCA.

24. Entries, 1826–1827, Nichols Academy Cash Book, 1819–1828, NCA.

25. *Catalogue . . . Nichols Academy . . . 1850–1851*, NCA.

26. Ibid., 1859–1860.

27. Robert R. Ducharme, comp. *Men Who Served From the Town of Dudley in the Civil War* (typescript, n.d.), 1.

28. *Catalogue . . . Nichols Academy . . . 1846*, NCA; Ibid.; 1851.

29. *Catalogue . . . Leicester Academy, Massachusetts, ending August 11, 1852* (Worcester: Henry J. Howland, 1852), 7–14.

30. Article 6, "*Constitution of Nichols Academy*," Dudley, Mass., 1819, NCA.

31. Nichols Academy Board of Trustees Meeting Minutes, November 28, 1823, NCA.

32. Ibid., August 29, 1827, NCA.

33. Record of Proceeding of the Board of Trustees of Nichols Academy, December 20 1822, Minutes of Board of Trustees, NCA.

34. Nichols Academy Board of Trustees Meeting Minutes, February 20, 1828, NCA.; Ibid., April 9, 1828. In fact, the town approved $250 to assist in these projects.

35. Ibid. This group included the *Massachusetts Spy, Boston Courier*, a Southbridge paper, and the Brooklyn, Connecticut, paper.

36. *Constitution of Nichols Academy*, NCA.

37. *Catalogue . . . Nichols Academy . . . 1855–1856*, 11.

38. Durnin, "New England's Eighteenth Century's Incorporated Academies," 73.

39. Sizer, *Age of the Academies*, 31–32.

40. Miller, *A Light on the Hill*, 11.

41. Ammidown, *Historical Collections*, II:60.

42. School Committee to the Town of Dudley, in Dudley Town Meeting Minutes, March 4, 1839, Town Meeting Records, 1794–1845, microfilm, FHL 861113, Genealogical Society of Utah, Salt Lake City, Utah, 1971.

43. Noble, *A History of American Education*, 109.

44. Cubberley, *Public Education*, 300.

45. Nichols Academy Board of Trustees Meeting Minutes, December 24, 1828, NCA.

46. Ibid. Town of Dudley Meeting Minutes, March 2, 1829, Dudley Town Meeting Records, 1794–1845, microfilm, FHL 861113, Genealogical Society of Utah, Salt Lake City, Utah, 1971.

47. *Catalogue . . . Nichols Academy . . . 1834; Catalogue . . . Nichols Academy . . . 1835.*

48. *Catalogue . . . Leicester Academy, For the Year Ending August 8, 1848* (Andover: William H. Wardwell, 1848), 15.

49. For more on the relationships between academies and colleges, see Marr, *Old New England Academies*, 37–67.

50. Cubberley, *Public Education in the United States*, 250.

51. "Textbooks," *Catalogue . . . Nichols Academy . . . 1850.*

52. *Catalogue . . . Nichols Academy . . . 1845.*

53. Ibid.

54. Marr, *Old New England Academies*, 236.

55. *Catalogue . . . Nichols Academy . . . 1846*.

56. *Catalogue . . . Nichols Academy . . . 1860*.

57. Willard S. Elsbree, *The American Teacher: Evolution of a Profession in a Democracy* (Westport, Conn.: Greenwood Press, 1970), 141.

58. Wilson Smith, *Theories of Education in Early America, 1655–1819* (Indianapolis and New York: Bobbs-Merrill Company, Inc., 1973), 345.

59. Copy of letter, Nichols to Turner, May 1, 1821, NCA.

60. Marr, *Old New England Academies*, 208.

61. See Wilson Smith, ed., *Theories of Education in Early America, 1655–1819* (Indianapolis and New York: The Bobbs-Merrill Company, 1973), 266.

62. Marr, *Old New England Academies*, 214–215.

63. *Constitution of Nichols Academy, 1819*, NCA.

64. Ibid.

65. *Catalogue . . . Nichols Academy . . . 1835*, 12.

66. Marr, *The Old New England Academies*, 69.

67. Ibid., 68.

68. Ibid.

69. Nichols Academy Board of Trustees Minutes, June 30, 1849, NCA.

70. *Constitution of Nichols Academy 1819*, NCA.

71. Durnin, "New England's Eighteenth Century Incorporated Academies," 166–167.

72. Nichols Academy Board of Trustees Meeting Minutes, February 20, 1828. Also see *Massachusetts Spy*, March 5, 1828.

73. Catalogue . . . Nichols Academy . . . 1834, used with permission of the American Antiquarian Society.

74. Smith, "Survival of an Old New England Academy," 98.

75. Christopher P. Bickford, *Plainfield Transformed: Three Centuries of Life in a Connecticut Town, 1699–1999* (Plainfield, Conn.: Plainfield Historical Society, 1999), 82.

76. Nichols Academy Board of Trustees Meeting Minutes, February 18, 1845, NCA.

77. *Catalogue . . . Nichols Academy . . . 1845*, NCA; Ibid., 1846.

78. Ibid., 1846.

79. Nichols Academy Board of Trustees Meeting Minutes, June 29, 1850, NCA.

80. *Catalogue . . . Nichols Academy . . . 1850*, NCA; Ibid., 1851; Ibid., 1852.

81. Nichols Academy Board of Trustees Meeting Minutes, June 25, 1853.

82. Ibid., June 26, 1852, NCA.

83. Nichols Academy Board of Trustees Meeting Minutes, November 21, 1856, NCA.

84. *Catalogue . . . Nichols Academy . . . 1857–1858*, NCA.

85. Ibid.

86. Ibid., 1858–1862.

87. Ibid., . . . 1861–1862, NCA.

88. Refer to Nichols Academy Board of Trustees Meeting Minutes, 1825–1860, NCA.

CHAPTER 3 ∼ A TASTE FOR IMPROVEMENT

1. Kaestle, *Pillars of the Republic*, 102.

2. Ibid., 152.

3. Rev. Zephaniah Baker, "Dudley," in *History of Worcester County, Massachusetts* (Boston: C. F. Jewett & Company, 1879), I:430–443.

4. *Catalogue . . . Nichols Academy . . . 1860–61*, 12, NCA.

5. Nichols Academy Board of Trustees Meeting Minutes, August 16, 1851, NCA.

6. Laws of Massachusetts, June 18, 1819, May, 1819 – February, 1822, 242. Also see *Constitution, Nichols Academy, 1819*, NCA.

7. Kaestle, *Pillars of the Republic*, 152–160.

8. *Massachusetts Spy*, March 5, 1828, courtesy American Antiquarian Society.

9. Nichols Academy Board of Trustees Meeting Minutes, August 28, 1839, NCA.

10. *Catalogue . . . Nichols Academy . . . 1841*, NCA.

11. Ibid., 1855–56, 10.

12. Kaestle, *Pillars of the Republic*, 188.

13. Sherman M. Smith, *The Relations of the State to Religious Education in Massachusetts* (Syracuse, N.Y.: Syracuse University Bookstore, 1926), 94.

14. Durnin, "New England's Eighteenth-Century Incorporated Academies," 147–148.

15. Marr, *Old New England Academies*, 106. See also Margaret A. Nash, *Women's Education in the United States, 1780–1840* (New York: Palgrave Macmillan, 2005), 1–10.

16. Nash, *Women's Education in the United States*, 1780–1840, 3.

17. Entries, 1819–1827, Nichols Academy Cash Book, 1819–1828, NCA.

18. Ibid., Entries, 1828.

19. Ibid., Entries, 1820–1828.

20. Nichols Academy Catalogues, 1835–1860, NCA.

21. *Worcester Spy*, March 5, 1828.

22. Nichols Academy Board of Trustees Meeting Minutes, April 9, 1828, NCA.

23. Dolly Corbin's workbook is available in the Old Sturbridge Village Library, Sturbridge, Massachusetts.

24. Marr, *Old New England Academies*, 202.

25. Entries, 1822, 1825, Nichols Academy Cash Book, 1819–1828, NCA.

26. *Catalogue . . . Nichols Academy . . . 1835*, NCA.

27. *Catalogue . . . Nichols Academy . . . 1855–1856*, NCA; Ibid., 1850–1851; Ibid., *1860–1861*.

28. *Catalogue . . . Nichols Academy . . . 1857–1858*, 7, NCA.

29. Cubberley, *Public Education*, 251.

30. Goodell, *Black Tavern Tales*, 32.

31. Anson and Edwin Goodell to "Dear Mother and Father," (Warren Goodell & Clarinda Healy Goodell), Nov. 14, n.y,. in Anson Goodell Letters, Black Tavern Historical Society, Dudley, Mass.

32. Ibid.

33. Goodell, *Black Tavern Tales*, 32.

34. *Catalogue . . . Nichols Academy . . . 1860–1861*, NCA.

35. Marr, *Old New England Academies*, 136–144.

36. Ibid., 144.

37. Goodell, *Black Tavern Tales*, 43.

38. John Thorn, "The Game That Got Away," *Boston Sunday Globe*, July 10, 2005, E1–3.

39. Jim Douglas, "True Colors," *Nichols College Magazine*, Vol. 8, Issue No. 2, Fall-Winter 2013, 17.

40. Goodell, *Black Tavern Tales*, 43–44.

41. This reference is to a book by Charles Carleton Coffin, *The Boys of '61, or, Four years of fighting, personal observation with the army and the navy, from the first battle of Bull Run to the fall of Richmond* (Boston: Estes and Lauriat, 1896).

42. Goodell, *Black Tavern Tales*, 44.

43. *Academy Bell* (May 1905), II:38.

44. Goodell, *Black Tavern Tales*, 32–33.

45. Marr, *Old New England Academies*, 120. See also Nichols Academy Catalogues. 1834–1880.

46. *Catalogue . . . Nichols Academy . . . 1834*, courtesy American Antiquarian Society. Mrs. Nancy Day rented the Academy for twenty dollars a term. See Nichols Academy Board of Trustees Meeting Minutes, August, 1834, NCA.

47. Goodell, *Black Tavern Tales*, 29–30.

48. *Catalogue . . . Nichols Academy . . . 1861–1862*, NCA; *Catalogue . . . Nichols Academy . . . 1850–1851*, NCA.

49. Christopher P. Bickford, *Plainfield Transformed*, 82; *Catalogue . . . Leicester Academy . . . 1848*, 5.

50. Joseph Murphy et al, *The Productive High School: Creating Personalized Academic Communities* (Thousand Oaks, California: Corwin Press, Inc. 2001), 6.

51. Account of boarding, Nichols Academy, 1825, NCA. Several of Samuel Slater's older sons had attended The Episcopal Academy of Connecticut at Cheshire, Connecticut. See E.H. Cameron, *Samuel Slater: Father of American Manufactures* (Portland, Maine: The Bond Wheelwright Company, 1960), 123–129.

52. *Catalogue . . . Nichols Academy . . . 1841 for the year ending August 24, 1841*, 10, NCA; *Catalogue . . . Nichols Academy . . . 1851*.

53. Goodell, *Black Tavern Tales*, 29.

54. Bickford, *Plainfield Transformed*, 81–82.

55. United States Bureau of the Census, *Historical Statistics of the United States: Colonial Times to 1970*, Part I (Washington, D.C.: U.S. Dept. of Commerce, Bureau of the Census, 1976), 163–165.

56. Copy of letter, Nichols to Turner, May 1, 1821, NCA.

57. For a sample of these notices, see *Worcester Spy*, March 5, 1828.

58. Nichols Academy Board of Trustees Meeting Minutes, August 2, 1838, NCA.

59. *Catalogue . . . Nichols Academy . . . 1844–45*, 8–10, NCA.

60. Ibid., *1849–1850*, 11, NCA; also see *Catalogue . . . Nichols Academy . . .1855–1856*, 9–11.

61. This is a situation similar to that experienced by Exeter Academy as described by James McLachlan in *American Boarding Schools*, 47.

62. *Catalogue . . . Nichols Academy . . . 1859–1860*, 9, NCA.

63. Joshua Bates, D.D., "Topographical and Historical Notices of the Town of Dudley, Mass." in *An Anniversary Discourse, Delivered at Dudley, Mass., March 20, 1853* (Boston: T.R. Marvin, 42 Congress Street, 1853), 55–57. His granddaughter, Katharine Lee Bates, wrote the words of "America the Beautiful." See Moseley, *250 Years, 1721–1982*, 19.

64. McLachlan, *American Boarding Schools*, 45.

65. Edwin D. Sanborn, "An Oration Delivered Before the Alumni of Gilmanton Academy, August 4, 1859," quoted in Durnin, "New England's Eighteenth-Century Incorporated Academies," 234.

CHAPTER 4 ∼ A NEW ACADEMY EMERGES

1. The term, "mixed corporation" is suggested by McLachlan, *American Boarding Schools*, 221.

2. http://stevepayne.home.mindspring.com/ps03/ps03_096.htm [accessed March 24, 2007].

3. Marr, *Old New England Academies*, 88.

4. *Catalogue . . . Nichols Academy . . . 1850*; Ibid., 1851.

5. Ibid., 1851; Ibid., 1852.

6. Marr, *Old New England Academies*, 71.

7. *Catalogue . . . Nichols Academy . . .1858*, 7, NCA.

8. Ibid., 1860, 9.

9. Ibid.

10. Ibid., 1860–61, 12–13; Ibid., 1863, 18.

11. Ibid., 1858, 7.

12. Ibid., 1861, 12.

13. Refer to Nichols Academy *Catalogues* from 1857 to 1863.

14. Ibid.

15. Goodell, *Black Tavern Tales*, 30.

16. *Catalogue. . . Nichols Academy . . . 1860–61*, 10; Ibid., *1861–1862*, 14; Ibid., *1862–1863*, 5–15.

17. Refer to Henry S. Burrage, *Brown University in the Civil War: A Memorial: 1868* (Providence: Providence Press Company, 1868) 93–108; Robin Young, *For Love & Liberty: The Untold Civil War Story of Major Sullivan Ballou and His Famous Love Letter* (New York: Thunder's Mouth Press, 2006). For a detailed story of Ballou's last hours, see Evan C. Jones, "The Macabre Fate of Sullivan Ballou," *America's Civil War Magazine* (November 2004).

18. According to Civil War researcher, Robert Ducharme, 149 Union soldiers and sailors can be identified as coming from Dudley. Twenty-nine are known to have died in battle or from wounds or disease. This included six who attended the Academy. See Robert R. Ducharme, comp., "Men who served the Town of Dudley in the Civil War," (Typescript, n.d.).

19. *Putnam Patriot*, September 11, 1903; "George Whitefield Davis," *The Twentieth Century Dictionary of Notable Americans* (Boston, MA: The Biographical Society, 1904), III:157.

20. Theodore Tilton, "Victoria Woodhull, A Biographical Sketch," *The Golden Age* tract no. 3 (New York: 1871), http://victoria-woodhull.com/tiltonbio.htm, 10/ [accessed April 21, 2007].

21. Lois B. Underhill, *The Woman Who Ran For President: The Many Lives of Victoria Woodhull* (Bridgehampton, N.Y.; Bridge Works Publishing Company, 1995), 38; Amanda Frisken, *Victoria Woodhull's Sexual Revolution: Political Theater and the Popular Press in Nineteenth-Century America* (Philadelphia: University of Pennsylvania Press, 2004), ix.

22. Mary Gabriel, *Notorious Victoria: The Life of Victoria Woodhull, Uncensored* (Chapel Hill: Algonquin Books, 1998), 29–30, 269.

23. Underhill, *The Woman Who Ran For President*, 36.

24. Gabriel, *Notorious Victoria*, 198–228.

25. Ibid., 262.

26. Nichols Academy Board of Trustees Meeting Minutes, March 4, 1864, NCA.

27. Ibid., May 23, 1863.

28. Worcester County Registry of Deeds, 778:512; Nichols Academy Board of Trustees Meeting Minutes, June 28, 1868, NCA.

29. Registry of Deeds, Worcester County Court House, Worcester, Mass., December 17, 1867, 778:512.

30. Nichols Academy Board of Trustees Meeting Minutes, June 26, 1869, NCA.

31. *Webster Times*, April 2, 1870.

32. Nichols Academy Board of Trustees Meeting Minutes, May 22, 1869, NCA.

33. Ibid., June 26, 1869.

34. Ibid., February 26, 1869; Ibid., June 6, 1869. Dudley Town Meeting Minutes, April 5, 1869; Ibid., April 17, 1869.

35. Label on Students' Grade Reports, "Nichols Academy and High School," 1894–1897, folder #19, NCA.

36. Grizzell, *Origin and Development of the High School in New England*, 86–87.

37. Ibid., 31.

38. McLachlan, *American Boarding Schools*, 45.

39. Nichols Academy Board of Trustees Meeting Minutes, May 12, 1871, NCA.

40. *Charter and Constitution of Nichols Academy; with notes from the Records* (1897), 22, NCA.

41. Grizzell, *Origin and Development of the High School in New England*, 144; Cubberley, *Public Education in the United States*, 257.

42. Dudley Town Meeting Minutes, April 3, 1871, Town Hall, Dudley, Massachusetts.

43. Ibid., August 11, 1871.

44. Worcester County Court House, Registry of Deeds, April 30, 1871, 850:286–289.

45. Nichols Academy Board of Trustees Meeting Minutes, May 5, NCA; Ibid., May 12, 1871.

46. Occasionally the state reminded the town of its obligations under the Act of 1827. See *Reports of Town Officers of the Town of Dudley for the Year ending 1881*, 10.

47. *Reports of the Town Officers and School Committee of the Town of Dudley, for the year 1871–1872* (Webster: Times Book and Job Office, 1872), 21.

48. Entry, October 7, 1871, Dr. A.M. Gory, Nichols Academy Treasurer's Book, 1824–1902, NCA.

49. Nichols Academy Board of Trustees Meeting Minutes, September 26, 1873, NCA.

50. Ibid., January 17, 1873.

51. Ibid., December 26, 1873.

52. "Report," Dudley School Committee, 1880–1881, 10.

53. Smith, "Survival of an Old New England Academy," 32.

54. *Farmer's Monthly Visitor* II (February 28, 1840), 18.

55. Interview, Mary Bair with author, June 27, 1995, VID 516–1, NCA.

56. Kaestle, *Pillars*, 103.

57. Grizzell, *Origin and Development of the High School*, 360.

58. Kaestle, *Pillars*, 103.

59. Altenbaugh, *American People and Their Education*, 80.

60. Butts and Cremin, *A History of Education in American Culture*, 209.

61. Rev. Calvin D. Hulbert, *The Academy: Demands for it, and the Conditions of its Success* (Boston: New-England Publishing Company, 1878), 6–27.

62. John R. Thayer, "*Seventh Annual Reunion of the Alumni of Nichols Academy, Dudley Mass.*, June 17, 1881 (Southbridge: Journal Steam Book Print, 1881), 25.

63. Marcellus Coggan, *Ninth Annual Reunion of the Alumni of Nichols Academy, Dudley, Mass., June 15th 1883* (Southbridge: Journal Steam Book Print, 1884), 24.

64. For more on this point, see Prude, *The Coming of Industrial Order*, 271–272.

65. This is suggested in the *Academy Bell*, June 17, 1904, 41, NCA.

66. Thayer, "Seventh Annual Reunion . . . Nichols Academy . . ." June 17, 1881, 25.

67. *Catalogue . . . Nichols Academy . . . 1872–1873* (Southbridge: Journal, n.d.), 14.

68. Frederick Odell Conant, *A History and Genealogy of the Conant Family* (Portland, Maine: Private print [Press of Harris and Williams], 1887), 465. Also see *A Souvenir of the Conant Memorial Church; Its Inception, Construction and Dedication; Printed for Hezekiah Conant* (Boston: Forbes Lithograph Manufacturing, 1893), 123–126.

69. Conant, *Genealogy*, 466–468.

70. Letter, John Bell to Thomas A. Jenckes, November 8, 1946, Thomas A. Jenckes Family Papers, Subgroup 8, box 24, folder 2, Rhode Island Historical Society Library, Providence, Rhode Island.

71. Dudley Town Meeting Minutes, November 14, 1831, Dudley, Massachusetts, microfilm, Dudley Town Meetings, 1793–1845, microfilm, FHL 86111, Item 1.

72. Ibid.

73. Ibid.

74. Bates, *Anniversary Discourse*, 51: U.S. Census, Dudley, Massachusetts, 1840.

75. www.capecodhistory.us/Mass1890/Dudley1890.htm [accessed April 16, 2004].

76. Address, Hezekiah Conant, *Ninth Alumni Reunion of the Alumni of Nichols Academy, Dudley, Mass.* (Southbridge: Journal Steam Book Press, 1884), 44.

77. It has to be noted again that Nichols Academy Board of Trustees Meeting Minutes between 1875 and 1915 are not with the Academy records in the Nichols College Archives. Whether or not these minutes still exist is questionable. However, in most instances, enough information is available through other Academy sources and local newspapers to complete the Academy's history over this period.

78. Worcester County Registry of Deeds, July 2, 1874, 935:338.

79. Ibid., 1003:321–322.

80. Address, Hezekiah Conant, *Seventh Annual Reunion of Nichols Academy, Dudley, Mass.*, June 17, 1881, 23, NCA. Also see *Webster Times*, June 24, 1881.

81. Dudley Town Meeting Minutes, April 5, 1880, Dudley Town Hall, Dudley, Mass.

82. *Webster Times*, June 26, 1880.

83. Ibid., June 24, 1881; Ibid., June 16, 1882.

84. "New Building," *Seventh Annual Reunion of the Alumni of Nichols Academy, Dudley, Mass., June 17, 1881* (Southbridge, Mass.: Journal Steam Book Print, 1881), backpage.; Hurd, *History of Worcester County, Massachusetts*, 2:1364. Also see Worcester Registry of Deeds, June 25, 1881, 1094:570–571.

85. Correspondence, C. L. Goodell, President of the Nichols Academy Board of Trustees, to Rev. Paul Rader, D.D., September 21, 1925, in Nichols Academy Board of Trustees Meeting Minutes, 1915–1971, NCA.

86. Address, Hezekiah Conant, *Seventh Annual Reunion of Nichols Academy, Dudley, Mass.*, June 17, 1881, 23, NCA. Also see *Webster Times*, June 24, 1881.

87. Worcester Registry of Deeds, June 25, 1881, 1094:570–571; Ibid., 1105:474–476.

NICHOLS ACADEMY: THE SPRING ON THE HILL 〜

88. *Webster Times*, June 24, 1881. The Dudley Town Meeting of November 2, 1880, had approved an Article authorizing the Selectmen "to draw from Contingent Fund the sum of 125 dollars for the purpose of hanging Memorial Tablets in the New Academy Hall." In June 1881, the Academy building was dedicated before what the *Massachusetts Weekly Spy* described as "one of the largest assemblages ever held in the town." The structure and land then were given to the Academy trustees by Hezekiah Conant. Details of the celebrations were reported in at least three local newspapers which mentioned the numerous speeches, toasts, and applause for Conant's great gift. Consistent with their wishes, the voters of Dudley saw the Memorial Tablets hung in the Academy's main hall. However, only the *Southbridge Journal* actually mentioned them. Even then, the reporter merely copied the Academy press release stating "In the main hall is the inscription 'erected by the people of Dudley in memory of her sons who died for the unity of the republic.' These contain a list of 27 names." The two main tablets were roughly four and half feet by two and a half feet. A third small tablet contained the inscription. The *Massachusetts Weekly Spy* featured the building's dedication in a front page, two-column piece, while the *Webster Times* used more than half of its front page to cover the story. Neither of these newspapers mentioned the Memorial Tablets.

89. Address, Hezekiah Conant, *Seventh Annual Reunion of Nichols Academy, Dudley, Mass.*, June 17, 1881, 23, NCA. Also see *Webster Times*, June 24, 1881.

90. Ibid.

91. Address, Hezekiah Conant, *Eighth Annual Reunion of the Alumni, Nichols Academy, Dudley, Mass.*, June 16, 1882 (Southbridge, Mass.: Journal Steam Book Print, 1882), 22.

92. *Webster Times*, June 16, 1882.

93. Worcester County Registry of Deeds, Worcester, Mass., October 3, 1900, 1665: 469–472.

94. Hurd, *History of Worcester County, Massachusetts* II:1364.

95. *Catalogue of Nichols Academy*, Dudley, Mass., 1885 (Southbridge: Herald Publishing Company, 1885), NCA. This catalogue incorrectly suggests that a James Clark gave the telescope to Conant. Later catalogues correct this mistake. It was James Coats, not James Clark, who gave the Clark telescope to Conant. A senior member of the firm of J. and P. Coats, Ltd., of Paisley, Scotland, a leading thread manufacturer, James Coats was working with Conant managing the Coats' interest in the Conant Thread Company. In 1891, the Conant Thread Company was dissolved and operated as a branch of J. and P. Coats. James Coats lived in Providence, R.I., and was a close associate of Conant.

96. Letter, Charles L. Goodell to the Editor, the *Nichols Budget*, October 16, 1934, NCA.

97. H. Conant, "*What I Know about the Vernal Equinox, its uses* (Pawtucket, R.I.: Adam Sutcliffe & Co., 1887), rear of back cover.

98. Hurd, *History of Worcester County, Massachusetts*, II:1364.

99. Patent for Astronomical Clock, March 9, 1887, to Hezekiah Conant of Pawtucket, Rhode Island, to United States Patent Office, October 11, 1887, U.S. Patent No. 371, 306, Folder #2508, NCA.

100. See *Catalogue . . . Nichols Academy . . . 1900–1901*, Dudley, Mass., 12, NCA. One Conant clock is in the Ladd Observatory, Brown University, Providence, R.I., while a third clock's location is unknown. For more on Conant clocks, see Philip Poniz, "An Extraordinary Tiffany & Co. Clock: Conant's Ingenious Regulator," www.antiquorum.com/html/vox/vox2004/tiffany.htm [accessed August 22, 2005].

101. Hezekiah Conant, *Eighth Annual Reunion of the Alumni of Nichols Academy, Dudley Mass., June 16, 1882*, (Southbridge: Journal Steam Book Print, 1882), 22.

102. *Webster Times*, May 15, 1885.

103. Ibid., June 4, 1886.

104. John R. Thayer, *Seventh Annual Reunion of the Alumni of Nichols Academy, Dudley, Mass., June 17, 1881* (Southbridge: Journal Steam Book Print, 1881), 26.

105. John R. Thayer, *Eighth Annual Reunion of the Alumni of Nichols Academy, Dudley, Mass., June 16, 1882* (Southbridge: Journal Steam Book Print, 1882), 25.

106. Clark Jillson, *Tenth Annual Reunion of Nichols Academy, Dudley, Mass., June 13, 1884* (Southbridge, Mass.: Journal Steam Book Press, 1884), 45.

CHAPTER 5 ~ THE NATURE OF MR. CONANT'S ACADEMY, 1874–1902

1. In his discussion of Exeter's Academy's alternatives during the period after 1880, James McLachlan found similar options. See McLachlan, *American Boarding Schools*, 220–221.

2. Unfortunately, the Minutes of Nichols Academy Board of Trustees Meetings between 1875 and 1915 are not available in the Nichols College Archives. However, the course of the Academy from 1875 to 1915 can be followed through other Academy documents, local newspapers and legal documents.

3. A general discussion of this process can be found in Joseph Murphy, et al, *The Productive High School: Creating Personalized Academic Communities* (Thousand Oaks, CA.: Corwin Press Inc., 2001), 22.

4. McLachlan, *American Boarding Schools*, 193.

5. Noble, *A History of American Education*, 314–315.

6. *Nichols Academy Announcement*, circa 1873–1876, NCA.

7. *Boston University Beacon*, April 26, 1876, Folder #502, NCA.

8. *Catalogue . . . Nichols Academy . . . 1875–1876* (Southbridge: Printed at the Journal Office), 11–13, NCA.

9. *Catalogue . . . Nichols Academy . . . Dudley, Mass., 1879–80*, 13, NCA; Ibid., 1884; Ibid., 1885; Ibid., 1889–1890.

10. "Announcement," Nichols Academy, 1878, NCA.

11. *Catalogue . . . Nichols Academy . . . Dudley, Mass., For Academic Year, 1872–73* (Southbridge: Journal Typography, n.d.), 8–14, NCA.

12. *Circular of Information of Nichols Academy for 1882–1883*, Dudley, Mass. (Webster: Times Office, n.d.), NCA.

13. *Catalogue . . . Nichols Academy . . . 1890*, 13, NCA.

14. *Annual Catalogue . . . Nichols Academy . . . 1896*, 14–21, NCA.

15. *Circular of Information of Nichols Academy, for 1882–1883*, Dudley, Mass. (Webster: "Times" Office, n.d.); also see *Catalogue of Nichols Academy, Dudley, Mass., 1884*, 9, NCA.

16. "Address," Hezekiah Conant, in "Exercises, 1886, "in *Graduation and Reunion of Alumni, 1886, 1887, 1888* (Webster: John Cort Printer, 1888), 41.

17. *Catalogue . . . Nichols Academy . . . 1886*, 11, NCA; Reunion Announcements, 1894, 1895, 1896, NCA.

18. *Annual Catalogue of the Officers and Students of Nichols Academy, Dudley, Mass., June 1896* (Pawtucket, R.I.: Adam Sutcliffe Co. Printers, 1896), 14, NCA.

19. Nichols Academy, "Principal's Report," Mr. & Mrs. E.P. Barker, November 21, 1879, NCA.

20. *Annual Catalogue of the Offices and Students of Nichols Academy, Dudley, Mass., June 1896* (Pawtucket, R.I.: Adam Sutcliffe Co. Printers, 1896), 13, NCA; Ibid., 1900–1901, 22. See also Thomas J. Schlereth, *Victorian America: Transformations in Everyday Life, 1876–1915* (New York: Harper Collins, 1991), 217–218.

21. *Annual Catalogue . . . Nichols Academy, Dudley, Mass., June 1890*, NCA; Ibid., June 1901, 30.

22. Nichols Academy, *Regulations to be Observed by Students* (Webster: John Cort, Printer and Stationer, 1878).

23. Nichols Academy, "Principal's Report for term ending November 21, 1879," NCA; Ibid., March 12, 1880.

24. Ibid., June 18, 1880.

25. Ibid., 1878–1901.

26. Ibid., 1884–1885, 1895–1896, 1900–1901.

27. Dudley Town Meeting Minutes, April 4, 1887, Town Clerk's Office, Dudley Town Hall, Dudley, Mass.

28. *Reports of the Town Officers and School Committee of the Town of Dudley for the year, 1871–1872* (Webster: Times Book and Job Offices, 1872), 20–21.

29. List, Receipts and Expenditures from the year ending June 21, 1895, Nichols Academy, NCA. Also refer to "Endowments," in *Catalogue . . . Nichols Academy . . . June 1901*, 22.

30. See "Principal's Report," for years 1893, 1894, 1895, 1899, 1900; NCA. Also refer to "List of Charlton Students," 1847–1905, Folder #2504, NCA. According to this list, 103 Charlton students attended Nichols Academy over this period.

31. *Annual Catalogue . . . Nichols Academy . . . Dudley, Mass., June 1896* (Pawtucket, R.I.: Adam Sutcliffe Co. Printers, 1896), 26, NCA.

32. Ibid., 1900–1901, 5.

33. Dudley Town Meeting Minutes, November 2, 1897, Town Clerk's Office, Dudley, Mass.

34. *Southbridge News*, June 29, 1877.

35. *Webster Times*, June 30, 1877.

36. Ibid.

37. Ibid.

38. *Southbridge News*, June 29, 1877. This account from the *Southbridge News* does not include any detailed references to class statistics.

39. Charles L. Robinson '84, "Nichols in the Eighties," *Nichols Alumnus*, Vol. 1, June 1947, No. 3, 1-2.

40. Ibid, 1-2.

41. Ibid.

42. Ibid.

43. Ibid.

44. Ibid.

45. Ibid.

46. Jack Fones '37, "Nichols Oldest Living Graduate, George James Searles '84," *Nichols Alumnus*, Vol. 1, October 1947, No. 4, 2.

47. Ibid.

48. Channing Wells '86, "Nichols Academy in 1886," *The Nichols Alumnus*, Vol. 2, June 1848, No. 3, 6.

49. Ibid., 6.

50. Ibid.

51. Ibid., 6.

52. Ibid., 4.

53. Ibid., 5.

54. Ibid.

55. *Webster Times*, September 26, 1931.

56. Ibid., 6.

57. *Representative Men and Old Families of Rhode Island*, I, (Chicago: J. H. Beers & Co., 1908), 70.

58. *National Cyclopaedia of American Biography*, 22: (New York: James T. White, 1932), 58.

59. Moseley, *250 Years 1732–1982*, 28.

60. For a sensitive and revealing portrait of Hezekiah Conant, see Samuel Morris Conant, "Intimate Sketch of his Father," *Webster Evening Times*, July 30, 1926.

61. *Academy Bell*, June 17, 1904, 41.

62. Reverend Charles L. Goodell, *My Mother's Bible: A Memorial Volume of Addresses for the Home*, 2nd ed. (Boston: Lee and Shepard Publishing, 1891), 125.

63. Moseley, *250 Years, 1732–1982*, 23.

64. *A Souvenir of the Conant Memorial Church* (Boston: Lithograph Mftg. Company for Hezekiah Conant, 1893), 13. For more on Hezekiah Conant and the First Congregational Church, see Marion Moseley, *250 Years, 1732–1982; First Congregational Church, Conant Memorial, Dudley, Mass.*, (Typescript, n.d.).

65. Donor's (Hezekiah Conant) Letter to the First Congregational Church and Society in Dudley, Mass., December 18, 1891, in *A Souvenir of the Conant Memorial Church*, 59.

66. Dudley Town Meeting Minutes, June 6, 1891, Town Clerk's Office, Dudley Town Hall, Dudley, Mass.

67. Washington Hall, standing where the new Center School was to be constructed, was moved to the north of the church and became the Grange Hall. Conant's selection of a new architect for the Church and Center School projects may have been due to the retirement of Elbridge Boyden in 1889.

68. *Webster Times*, October 2, 1880.

69. Conant, *Genealogy of the Conant Family*, 49.

70. *Report of the Town Officers of Dudley, for the year ending March 1, 1900*, 31.

71. Address, Hezekiah Conant, June 13, 1884, *Tenth Annual Reunion of the Alumni of Nichols Academy, Dudley, Mass., June 13, 1884* (Southbridge: Journal Steam Book Print, 1884), 45, NCA.

72. Nichols Academy Board of Trustees Meeting Minutes, May 22, 1875, NCA.

73. *Academy Bell*, January, 1904, I:4.

74. *Worcester Telegram*, December 15, 1929.

CHAPTER 6 ~ THE SEARCH FOR A LARGER FIELD OF USEFULNESS

1. McLachlan, *American Boarding Schools*, 193.

2. Letter, Reverend Goodell to *Webster Times*, March 13, 1923.

3. *Southbridge Press*, June 19, 1909. Also see *Webster Times*, June 17, 1909.

4. "Principal's Report," 1898–1899, 1900–01, NCA.

5. *Souvenir Edition, Webster Times*, 1905, 19.

6. *Webster Times*, September 26, 1931.

7. *Academy Bell*, September 1904, 65; Ibid., January 1904, 5. The Academy Catalogue of 1907 and 1908 also referred to a "football" team. Also see *Annual Catalogue . . . Nichols Academy, Dudley, Mass., 1907–1908*, 8, NCA.

8. *Announcement of the Ninetieth Year of Nichols Academy, 1904–05*, NCA.

9. F. C. Johnson to E. W. Robinson, n.d., in "Dudley School Reports, 1905," 17, in *Reports of the Town Officers of Dudley for the Year ending March 1, 1905* (Webster: Webster Press, 1905).

10. "Announcement," Nichols Academy, 1904–1905, NCA.

11. Theodore Sizer, *Secondary Schools at the Turn of the Century* (New Haven, CT: Yale University Press, 1964), 132, quoted in Murphy et al, *Productive High School*, 22.

12. Samuel W. Hallett to Ernest W. Robinson, January 1, 1906, in "Dudley School Report, 1906, 21–23, in *Reports of the Town Officers of Dudley for the Year ending March 1, 1906* (Webster: Webster Press, 1906).

13. Ibid. Also see "Annual Report of the School Committee for the Year Ending March 1, 1907," 29–31, in *Report of the Officers of Dudley for the Year Ending March 1, 1907* (Webster: Webster Press, 1907).

14. Letter, Hallett to Robinson, n.d., in "Dudley School Report, 1908," 27–29, in *Report of the Officers of Dudley for the Year Ending March 1, 1908* (Webster: Webster Press, n.d.).

15. *Annual Catalogue . . . Nichols Academy . . . Dudley, Massachusetts, 1907–1908*, (Academy: Davis Press, June 1907), NCA.

16. Letter, Ernest T. Chase to E.W. Robinson, n.d., "Report of the School Committee, March 1, 1909," 20–23, in *Report of the Town Officers of Dudley, for the Year ending March 1, 1909*.

17. Superintendent's Report in *Annual Report* of the School Committee, March 1, 1909, in *Report of the Town Officers of Dudley for the Year Ending March 1, 1909* (Webster: Webster Press, 1909).

18. Ibid. Some students who went to high school in Webster were required to take a sub-freshman year.

19. The Nichols Academy Trustee Meetings Minutes for the period 1875–1915 are not available.

20. An interesting parallel to the Nichols experience can be found in the history of Phillips Exeter Academy in New Hampshire. During the 1880s, Exeter was debating its future and had to redefine its goals. After much consideration and debate, it emerged as a true boarding school and worked to house all students in dormitories, increase teachers' salaries, and raise tuition. Like Nichols, Exeter had been hampered by the low standards in its basic English course. As a result, the school focused solely on a college preparatory program and expanded successfully. One examination of academies concludes that some nineteenth century academies had to become expensive boarding schools to survive. See McLachlan, *American Boarding Schools*, 219–241.

21. Refer to "Principal's Report," 1900–1901, NCA; Commencement Exercises of Nichols Academy and Twenty-Fourth Reunion of the Alumni, June 22, 1900, NCA; Commencement Exercises and Alumni Reunion, Class of 1902, June 20, 1902, NCA; Twenty-Eighth Annual Reunion of the Alumni of Nichols Academy, Dudley, Mass., June 17, 1904, NCA; Program of Commencement Exercises, Nichols Academy, Dudley, Mass., 1907, June 9, 1907, NCA. See the *Southbridge Press*, June 11, 1909; *Webster Times*, June 17, 1909.

22. Smith, "The Survival of an Old New England Academy," 191–197.

23. *Leicester's 250th Anniversary, 1722–1972; Leicester, Massachusetts, 1722–1972: A Look at the Past* (1972), n.p.

24. Report, E. W. Robinson, Dudley superintendent of schools, in "Annual Report of the School Committee . . . for the Year Ending March 1, 1910," 21–22, in *Report of the Town Officers of Dudley For the Year Ending March 1, 1910* (Webster: Webster Press, 1910).

25. *Webster Times*, June 10, 1909.

26. This is one newspaper's conclusion, but probably it is correct. Also see the *Southbridge Herald*, June 10, 1909.

27. "Report," E. W. Robinson, Dudley superintendent of schools, in *Annual Report of the School Committee: for Year Ending March 1, 1910*, 18, in *Report of the Town Officers of Dudley for the Year Ending March 1, 1910* (Webster: Webster Press, 1910).

28. *Report of School Committee of Dudley, for 1909–1910*, 10, in *Annual Report of the School Committee: for Year Ending March 1, 1910*, 10, in *Report of the Town Officers of Dudley for the Year Ending March 1, 1910* (Webster: Webster Press, 1910).

29. Dudley School Committee to Nichols Academy Trustees, 1912, Folder #1, NCA.

30. Dudley Town Meeting Minutes, August 8, 1916, Dudley Town Clerk's Office, Dudley, Mass.

31. *School Committee Reports, 1908–1910.* "Annual School Report, Dudley, June 1914 to June 1915," in *Reports, Town of Dudley*, for the year ending February 1, 1916, 7, 30.

32. Dudley Town Meeting Minutes, June 3, 1915; Letter, Frederick Thayer to E. W. Robinson, superintendent, Dudley Schools, November 3, 1915, Nichols Academy Trustee Minutes, 1915–1971, NCA.

33. Nichols Academy Board of Trustees Meeting Minutes, July 2, 1915, NCA.

34. Ibid., July 21, 1917.

35. See "Reports of School Board," Dudley, from 1916–1923, in *Reports of the Town of Dudley*. See also *Webster Times*, March 1, 1923, 1, 5.

36. Dudley School Committee Reports, 1920–1926.

37. Letter, Chase to Robinson, in *Report of the School Committee of Dudley, March 1,1909*, 20.

38. Reports of the Town Officers of Dudley, for the year March 1, 1901 (Webster: Webster Times, 1901), 135–137.

39. Letter, Dudley School Committee to Nichols Academy, 1912, in Nichols Academy Package #1, folder #1, NCA.

40. Nichols Academy Board of Trustees Meeting Minutes, 1918–1921, NCA.

41. *Webster Times*, December 18, 1922; Ibid., January 11, 1923; Ibid., February 22, 1923, 8; Unsigned agreement, Trustees of Nichols Academy and Bethel Bible Institute, February 24, 1923, NCA; Worcester County Registry of Deeds, March 16, 1923, 2293:261.

42. Nichols Academy Board of Trustees Meeting Minutes, December 8, 1922, NCA.

43. Ibid.

44. Letter, Goodell to *Webster Times*, March 13, 1923, NCA.

45. Worcester County Registry of Deeds, March 23, 1923, 2293:261–261.

46. Ibid. Also see *Webster Times*, March 15, 1923.

47. "Constitution of Bethel Bible Institution, Inc.," December 19, 1909, Folder #2511, NCA.

48. *Webster Times*, May 31, 1923.

49. http://www.gordon.edu/page.cfm?iPageID=377&iCategoryID=31&About& History_of_Barrington_College <http://www.gordon.edu/page.cfm?iPageID= 377&iCategoryID=31&About&History_of_Barrington_College> [accessed December 29, 2007].

50. *Worcester Telegram*, June 26, 1923.

51. *Webster Times*, May 31, 1923.

52. Ibid., September 2, 1923.

53. Nichols Academy Board of Trustees Meeting Minutes, July 6, 1923, NCA.

54. Letter, Goodell to the *Webster Times*, March 13, 1923. See also unsigned agreement dated February 24, 1923, Nichols Academy and Bethel Bible Institute, Folder #2408, NCA. This document refers to the new institution as "Nichols Academy and Dudley Bible Institute." Apparently this designation later was changed as noted in Reverend Goodell's letter.

55. Nichols Academy Board of Trustees Meeting Minutes, February 24, 1923, NCA.

56. Nichols Academy Board of Trustees Meeting Minutes, August 10, 1925, NCA; Ibid., September 15, 1925; Letter, C.L. Goodell to Rev. Paul Rader, D.D., September 21, 1925, in volume of Nichols Academy Board of Trustees Meeting Minutes, 1915–1971, NCA.

57. Nichols Academy Board of Trustees Meeting Minutes, September 10, 1926, NCA.

58. *Worcester Telegram*, December 15, 1929.

59. Letter, Selectmen of Dudley to Board of Trustees, Nichols Academy, February 26, 1924. NCA; Ibid., May 22, 1924.

60. Nichols Academy Board of Trustees Meeting Minutes, January 8, 1927, NCA; Dudley Town Meeting Minutes, March 19, 1927, NCA; *Webster Times*, March 21, 1927.

61. "Report of the School Committee, Town of Dudley, Massachusetts, for the Year Nineteen Hundred Thirty-One," 4, in *Annual Reports of the Town Officers of the Town of Dudley, Massachusetts, for the year ending December 31, 1931* (Webster: Times Publishing Co., 1932).

62. "Town Warrant," Article 23, in *Annual Reports of the Town Officers of the Town of Dudley, Massachusetts, for the year ending December 31, 1926* (Webster: Times Publishing, 1927), 7.

63. Nichols Academy Board of Trustees Meeting Minutes, September 8, 1927, NCA.

64. Ibid., September 10, 1926.

65. Treasurer's Annual Report of the Trustees of Nichols Academy, July 9, 1927 to July 20, 1928, in Nichols Academy Board of Trustees Meeting Minutes, 1915–1971, NCA.

66. Nichols Academy Board of Trustees Meeting Minutes, special meeting, December 6, 1930, NCA.

67. Ibid., September 14, 1929.

68. Auditor's Report, Nichols Academy Board of Trustees Meeting, July 2, 1915, NCA.

69. Leslie R. Bragg, M.D., *The Doctors of Dudley and Webster, Massachusetts* (n.p.: Leslie Bragg, n.d.), 154–155; *Webster Times*, April 1, 1931.

70. Nichols Academy Board of Trustees Meeting Minutes, March 24, 1931, NCA.

71. *Fitchburg Sentinel*, April 3, 1931. Also see Fred (Friendly) Wachenheimer, "Quincy H. Merrill Instrumental in Founding of Nichols College," in *The Nichols Budget*, October 14, 1935, NCA; *The Nichols Budget*, October 5, 1936.

72. Worcester County Registry of Deeds, 2556:84–85; 2557:64; 2547:26–27, 28–29.

73. Form of Votes for Record of Meeting of Trustees of Nichols Academy held April 21, 1931, in Nichols Academy Board of Trustees Meeting Minutes, 1915–1971, NCA. Worcester County Registry of Deeds, 2547:221–222. This property was immediately mortgaged by the Nichols Academy Trustees to acquire additional funds. Ibid., July 29, 1931, 2547:224–226.

74. Form of Votes for Record of Meeting of Trustees of Nichols Academy Held April 21, 1931, in Nichols Academy Board of Trustees Meeting Minutes, 1915–1971, NCA.

75. Nichols Academy Board of Trustees Meeting Minutes, March 24, 1931, NCA.

76. Indenture, Trustees of Nichols Academy to Frederick Smith and James L. Conrad, August 20, 1931, Folder #20, NCA.

77. *Webster Evening Times*, April 1, 1931.

78. Worcester County Registry of Deeds, April 6, 1942, 2850:363.

79. Murphy et al, *The Productive High School*, 22–23.

80. Ibid., 32–33.

APPENDIX A

List of Nichols Academy Trustees, 1819–1931

	Yrs. Served		Yrs. Served
Jonathan Davis	1819–1832	George Slater	1833–1844
Amasa Nichols	1819–1823	Samuel Paine	1833–1844
Luther Ammidown	1819–1826	Peter Bacon	1833–1842
Isaiah Rider	1819–1820	Morris Larned	1834–
John Spurr	1819–1826	Chester Clemans	1834–1838
John Brown	1819–1834	Rev. James Francis	1836–1838
Rev. Hosea Ballou	1819–1820	Rev. John Boyden Jr.	1836–1840
Rev. Paul Dean	1819–1836	Rev. Hezekiah Davis	1836–1844
Dan Lamb	1819–1822	Theodore Leonard	1838–1845
Rev. Edward Turner	1819–1923	Rev. Walter Follet	1838–1844
Rev. Thomas Jones	1819–1821	Hammond Healy	1838–
Abraham R. Thompson	1819–1822	David Kingsbury	1838–
John Kettell	1819–1823	Lemuel Healy Jr.	1840–
Benjamin Russell	1819–1823	Rev. Joshua Britton	1840–1844
Benjamin Gleason	1819–1822	Loomis G. Leonard	1840–1845
Rev. John Bisbe	1820–1822	William Healy Jr.	1842–
Jeremiah Kingsbury	1821–1844	Ebenezer Davis	1843–
James Walcott, Jr.	1821–1823	Rev. Joshua Bates	1844–
Richard Olney	1822–1823	Allen Hancock Jr.	1844–
Ira Barton	1822–1834	Rev. Joseph Skinner	1844–
Samuel Slater	1822–1836	Amasa Davis 2d	1844–
William Winsor	1823–1838	John Eddy	1846–
William Hancock	1823–1845	Rev. Samuel Brimblecom	1846–
George Tufts	1823–1835	Rev. Jeremiah Hannaford	1846–
Jeptha Bacon	1823–1833	John Jewett	1846–
William Larned	1823–	Phineas Bemis	1851–1863
Rev. Abiel Williams	1823–1850	William Larned	
Rev. Ebenezer Newhall	1826–1839	D. Dorchester	
Linus Child	1827–1838	Rev. Henry Pratt	
Ebenezer Ammidown	1828–1833	David Dwight	1859–

Continued

List of Nichols Academy Trustees, 1819-1931 *Continued*

	Yrs. Served		*Yrs. Served*
Rev. Jacob Baker		George Thornton	1891
Alden Southworth		Eben Stevens	1899
Zephaniah Baker		Rufus Dodge	
Rev. Joseph Barber		Frederick Thayer	
Nelson Bennett		Dr. Edward R Miller	
George Davis		Dr. Fred G. Hart	
Oscar Chase	1863–	Ernest W. Robinson	
J. A. Spaulding	1864–	Zelotes W. Coombs	1908
Jacob Baker	1865–	John B. Williams	1915
Edwin May		Morris F. Conant	1915
Lemuel Healy		George B. Williams	
Charles E. Kimball		Charles L. Robinson	
John E. Edmunds		Rev. Ernest B. Patten	
Alexander DeWitt		William F. Sims	
Rev. F .E. Bacheler		George B. Hunt	
William S. Slater		Perry Parsons	
D. B. Kingsbury		Ralph Easterbrooks	
Oscar Fisher		George Hall	
James Robinson	1866–	Albert T. Stearnes	
Waldo Healy	1866–	Rev. William Ganley	
Charles Babcock	1872–	Dr. Hart	
Hezekiah Conant	1874–	Dr. Quincy H. Merrill	
Elisha Phillips	1874–	Herbert F. Davison	
Moses Barnes Jr.	1874–	Chester F. Stacey	
Josiah Perry	1875–	Rev. John Moseley	
Chester Corbin	1875	George Jacobs	
George Hartwell	1876	Clarence N. Nash	
John Thayer	1876	Mary Babcock	
Rev. Charles Goodell	1876	James Lobban	1931
Clark Jillson	1880	Wadsworth Crawford	
Hezekiah Williams	1880	Fred E. Corbin	
J. H. Work	1881	Maude Marsh	
Gov. A. H Littlefield	1884	Clarence R. Fletcher	
George Welles	1888	Henry Babcock	
Monroe Ide	1888	H. Nelson Conant	
Calvin Paige	1890	Earl Goodell	
Samuel Morris Conant	1891	George B. Hawkes	
John S. Gould	1891	Mrs. Clarence Nash	1931

Sources: Nichols Academy *Catalogues*, 1934–1931; Minutes, Meetings, Nichols Academy, 1819–1931, with some exceptions.

APPENDIX B

List of Preceptors/Principals, Nichols Academy, 1819–1909

	Yrs. Served		*Yrs. Served*
Solomon L. Wilds	1819–22	Alden Southworth	1854–56
Isaac Webb	1822–24	Ogden Hall	1856–57
William Rockwell	1824–26	Monroe Nichols	1857–62
H. Lowndes Street	1826–28	John T. Clark	1862–66
William G. Learned	1828–29	F. C. Burnett	1866–67
Sanford Lawton	1829–32	Isaiah Trufant	1868–69
William S. Potter	1832–33	A. L. Blake/Pope	1869
Darius Ayres	1833–34	Henry Burt	1869
Benjamin Diefendorf	1834–36	Harold M. Wilder	1870–71
John Bowers	1836–37	A. H. Livermore	1871–72
Oscar Fisher	1837–39	L. E. Morse	1872
Henry C. Morse	1839–40	Marcellus Coggan	1873–79
Elisha W. Cook	1840–42	Edmund Barker &	
Henry C. Morse	1842–44	Susan Barker	1879–81
Samuel L. Bates	1844–46	H. L. Dawson	1881–83
Alden Southworth	1846–49	F. E. Corbin	1883–86
Alvin H. Washburn	1849–51	Emerson G. Clark	1886–89
William W. Birchard	1851–52	Alfred G. Collins	1889–1902
Alvin H. Washburn	1852	Franklin C. Johnson	1903–05
John H. Almy	1852–53	Samuel W. Hallett	1905–08
James A. Clark	1853–54	Ernest Tucker Chase	1908–09

Sources: Nichols Academy Board of Trustees, 1819–1874; *Nichols Academy Catalogues, 1834–1907; Nichols "Principal's Report,"* 1879–1903, NCA; Dudley School Committee "Reports," 1903–1910.

APPENDIX C

Nichols Academy Student Enrollment Numbers, 1819–1909

Last Term Ends	Total* Register	Different Scholars	Terms	Males Enrolled	Females Enrolled	Female Percent	Dudley Males	Dudley Females	Dudley Total	Dudley% of Total	Dudley Totals Recorded After 1898
1820	146	110	4	117	29	20%					
1821	113	94	4	88	25	22%					
1822	128	109	4	107	21	16%					
1823	137	113	4	98	39	28%					
1824	135	114	4	95	40	30%					
1825	127	102	4	96	32	24%					
1826	101	84	4	75	26	26%					
1827	95	79	4	67	28	29%			37	39%	
1828	121	106	4	71	50	41%			51	42%	
1829											
1830											
1831											
1832											
1833											
1834	74		4	49	25	27%			50	68%	
1835		114	4	63	51	45%	15	20	35	31%	
1836											
1837											
1838											
1839		126	4	69	57	45%					
1840		133	4	79	54	40%			55	41%	
1841		137	4	86	51	37%	28	22	50	36%	
1842											
1843		127		87	40	32%	31	23	54	43%	
1844											
1845		89	4	56	33	37%	22	18	40	45%	
1846		91	3	48	43	47%	21	20	41	44%	
1847											
1848											
1849											
1850		91	3	39	52	57%	16	38	54	59%	
1851	102	82	3	47	55	54%	25	33	58	57%	
1852	82	70	3	48	34	41%	28	25	53	27%	
1853	71										
1854											
1855											
1856		131	3	80	51	39%	44	22	66	50%	
1857											
1858	265	171	4	118	53	31%	44	28	72	42%	
1859											
1860	186	159	3	136	50	27%	62	29	91	48%	

*Total includes three terms with each term tabulated separately and then added together for the total registration of that year.

Continued

Nichols Academy Student Enrollment Numbers, 1819–1909 *Continued*

Last Term Ends	Total* Register	Different Scholars	Terms	Males Enrolled	Females Enrolled	Female Percent	Dudley Males	Dudley Females	Dudley Total	Dudley% of Total	Dudley Totals Recorded After 1898
1861	244	181	3	156	88	36%	50	36	86	35%	
1862	267	198	3	153	114	43%	53	31	84	31%	
1863	248		4	147	111	40%	55	47	102	39%	
1864	236										
1865											
1866	216			127	89	41%	41	54	95	44%	
1867											
1868											
1869											
1870											
1871											
1872											
1873	123	72	3	34	38	53%	23	21	44	61%	
1874		127	3	67	60	47%	24	21	45	35%	
1875											
1876		145	3	83	62	43%	23	24	47	32%	
1877											
1878											
1879	151		3	96	55	36%	44	27	71	48%	
1880	98		3	68	30	31%	26	19	45	46%	
1881	129		3	82	47	37%	28	42	70	54%	
1882	151		3			38%			84	56%	
1883	111		3	77	34	31%	29	18	47	51%	
1884	144	68	3	79	65	45%	49	47	96	60%	
1885	164	77	3	118	46	28%	68	41	109	67%	
1886	136	65	3	86	50	37%	51	25	76	56%	
1887	191		3	134	52	27%	70	44	114	60%	
1888	133		3	90	42	35%	37	33	70	53%	
1889	128		3	82	46	37%	49	33	82	65%	
1890	146	75	3	95	51	35%	61	41	102	70%	
1891	165		3	83	82	50%	61	65	126	76%	
1892	145		3	62	83	57%	31	45	76	52%	
1893	127		3	53	74	58%	32	42	74	58%	
1894	189		3	89	91	53%	50	71	121	64%	
1895	192		3	96	96	50%	56	75	131	68%	
1896	154	83	3	82	72	47%	64	55	119	77%	
1897	111		3	61	50	45%	47	31	78	70%	
1898	154		3	96	58	39%	47	37	84	55%	
1899	102		3	52	50	49%	23	46	69	68%	38
1900	119		3	61	58	48%	27	48	75	63%	29
1901	141	55	3	59	82	58%	30	65	95	67%	35
1902											40
1903											48
1904		33									24
1905											28
1906		27									34
1907											20
1908		16									23
1909											20

*Total includes three terms with each term tabulated separately and then added together for the total registration of that year.

Sources: Nichols Academy Cash Book, 1819–1828, NCA; Nichols Academy *Catalogues*, 1834–1876, NCA; Principal's Reports, 1879–1901, NCA; Dudley School Committee Reports, 1900–1912.

APPENDIX D

Towns Represented in Nichols Academy Student Body by Selected Years with Yearly Enrollment Totals (including percentages) based on the Total of Three Separate Term Registrations Taking Place Each Year

1826–1827		1861–1862		1884–1885	
MASSACHUSETTS		MASSACHUSETTS		MASSACHUSETTS	
Dudley	(23–29%)	Dudley	(77–31%)	Dudley	(109–67%)
Southbridge	(9–13%)	Webster	(20–08%)	Webster	(12–07%)
Oxford	(8–12%)	Southbridge	(11–05%)	Charlton	(12–07%)
Charlton	(5–05%)	Charlton	(10–05%)	Southbridge	(2–02%)
Sutton	(2–03%)	Douglas	(8–03%)	Sturbridge	(3–02%)
Uxbridge	(2–03%)	Sturbridge	(6–03%)	Oxford	(1–01%)
		Farnumsville	(2–01%)	Hopedale	(1–01%)
		Fiskdale	(2–01%)	Lowell	(1–01%)
CONNECTICUT		Millbury	(2–01%)		
Woodstocks	(9–13%)	Northampton	(2–01%)	CONNECTICUT	
Thompson	(2–03%)	Auburn	(2–01%)	New Boston	(5–03%)
Pomfret	(2–03%)			Thompson	(4–03%)
				Woodstock	(3–02%)
RHODE ISLAND		CONNECTICUT		Grosvenordale	(2–02%)
Smithfield	(2–03%)	Thompson	(25–10%)		
Pawtucket	(1–02%)	Woodstocks	(23–10%)	RHODE ISLAND	
Unlisted	(2–03%)	Pomfret	(8–08%)	Chepachet	(3–02%)
		Putnam	(4–02%)	Manville	(3–02%)
		Killingly	(3–01%)	Fisherville	(2–01%)
		Fisherville	(2–01%)		
		RHODE ISLAND			
		Pascoag	(3–01%)		
		Mapleville	(2–01%)		
		Providence	(2–01%)		
		Gloucester	(2–01%)		
		NEW YORK			
		Brooklyn	(8–03%)		
		LeRoy	(4–02%)		
		Eleven towns had one.	(13–05%)		

Sources: Nichols Academy Cash Book, 1819–1828, NCA; *Catalogue . . . 1861–1862*, NCA; Nichols Academy *Principal's Report*, 1884–1885, NCA.

INDEX